GERALD PR

Gerald Priestland
1927 and describes
School education – Charterhouse, Oxford and the BBC'. However, before becoming the BBC's Religious Affairs Correspondent in 1977 he served it as a foreign correspondent in New Delhi, Beirut, Paris and Washington, besides presenting news programmes on radio and television.

Brought up as a Public School Anglican he was confirmed an English Presbyterian and is now a member of the Religious Society of Friends (the Quakers). He is married to Sylvia Priestland, the printmaker and photographer. They have four large children, a basset hound and two oriental cats. Besides their home in North London they own an abandoned Methodist Sunday School near Land's End (which Gerald considers appropriate for a man in his position).

Unhappy away from the typewriter for long, he is the author of eight previous books and looks forward to writing several more now that he has escaped from the routine of daily journalism – he retired from the BBC in June 1982. His motto, borrowed from Beaumarchais: 'I laugh at everything for fear of weeping.'

By the same author

YOURS FAITHFULLY (Volumes One and Two)
- *Fount Paperbacks*

PRIESTLAND'S PROGRESS
- *BBC Publications*

GERALD PRIESTLAND
At Large

Volume Three of the 'Yours Faithfully' Collected Radio Talks

by

Gerald Priestland

By arrangement with the British Broadcasting Corporation

Collins

FOUNT PAPERBACKS

First published in 1983 by Fount Paperbacks, London
Second Impression March 1983

Made and printed in Great Britain by
William Collins Sons & Co Ltd, Glasgow

A. M. D. G.

Contents

Introduction

Among the more ludicrous events of 1981 was my election, by the kindly listeners of the BBC 'Today' programme, as runner-up to Prince Charles as Man of the Year. I was followed by Tony Benn, who was followed by the Pope.

I can only guess that the honour was mainly due to my exposure as writer and presenter of the series 'Priestland's Progress – A Plain Man's Journey Through The Christian Faith', which ran for a total of almost ten hours on BBC Radio 4 and sold widely in its book version. But I had already featured lower down the poll the previous year; so it may be that the Saturday morning 'Yours Faithfully' talks – of which this is the third collected volume – also had something to do with my rating.

In which case, while thanking my listeners, I have to reprimand them too. A hack journalist, living comfortably in London, is no object for admiration. Prince, politician and Pope are all more useful than Priestland. There are moments when I contemplate doing something disgraceful – committing some kind of nuisance in a public place, perhaps – in order to shake off the mantle of sanctity which has been hovering about my shoulders of late. No thank you, I do not fancy a bishopric. You must look elsewhere for your media guru. Perhaps my treasonable disloyalty to the government's Falklands Expedition (muffled and counterbalanced though it had to be) will have helped to shatter the halo.

And yet, trying to be objective about the success these talks have achieved, I must force myself to understand what is going on, for that is part of the job as Religious Affairs correspondent. I cannot help being aware that my work gets borrowed for sermons (you are most welcome to it, reverend fathers), and that many non-churchgoers listen with interest. Hundreds of them write to me as a result of what they hear, so that much of my time is occupied with a kind of ministry by post – something for which I am wholly untrained.

It is something which, by any standard but that of Christian caring, I ought not to be doing at all. The BBC has been paying me to make programmes, not answer letters about moral and theological problems: that should be the Church's work, not mine. And yet my correspondents will not turn to the Church, if they have one. I can only suppose that this is partly because they feel they know and trust me, and because it is less embarrassing to write to an invisible confidant than to speak, face to face, with a real, live priest in your own community. But it is partly, also, a measure of the extent to which the Church has lost contact with the people.

I think it is possible to exaggerate the extent to which, in Britain, it ever was in touch. A strong vein of secular scepticism runs throughout our history. It is also possible to be too pessimistic about the decline of religion in general. But the facts are that Britain is full of people with religious needs who will not go into the churches, and of churches which would like to minister to such people but do not know how to speak to them.

Somewhere in the middle is the religious broadcaster. Working alongside others in the business of communication–information–entertainment, he is very much in the world and knows how to pull its levers and switches. It is he or she who now occupies the public pulpit, rather than the priest. Being religiously inclined, she or he is anxious to serve God and glorify him; but as a public servant, the broadcaster is nervous of seeming to manipulate the public and of confusing the theology of any one church with the Will of God. We are in a position to thump the Gospel or plug the Vatican Line, but we have to be careful not to – for we should lose our credibility if we did. Whether it should be possible, in Britain, for individual churches to buy time on the air is another matter. At present it is illegal, and the United States example is not encouraging. Myself, I still believe in a unified, middle-of-the-road approach to religious broadcasting rather than a pluralistic one under which the churches would cancel out one another's voices and lead listeners off into separate corners. Broadcasting *has* a mission to the individual believer, but I think it should be ancillary to a congregation, not a substitute for one.

Yet, again, what do we do about those believers – many of whom will even call themselves Christians – who will not join a congregation, or deal with a set-apart ministry?

I write now purely on my own account, for by the time this book appears I shall have retired from the permanent staff of the BBC and 'gone freelance'. Immediately, I must add that this is not due to any discontent on either side. The BBC has been liberal in its treatment of me for more than thirty years; it is just that I now respond less briskly than I should to the alarums and excursions of everyday events, and would like the time to do fewer (perhaps bigger) things better, and pay more attention to my neglected family.

And can I honestly say that it is only the flesh that is weakening before the demands of the journalistic life? I have to admit that the spirit, too, would like to sit down and think a bit. Keen listeners may have noticed that 'Yours Faithfully' has been coming less often from scenes of action. In any case, the BBC has shown no interest in my continuing it on a freelance basis. But the air-time is not my property; there must be as many listeners who detest me as those who like me; and it may very well be that someone else should have a turn before I become a bore.

On my own account, then, I take leave to wonder whether there should not be some kind of 'Church of the Air' to which the unchurchable (and churchgoers, too, if they wished) could turn for information, advice and support. It might devise its own forms of worship, suited to the medium (indeed, some experiments have already been made), and it would certainly need a staff of counsellors to handle the mail. I can imagine it having a building of its own, perhaps one of the under-used Wren churches in the City of London, with studios and offices to which members of the public could come in person if they cared to. Branches might well develop in other centres. Finance might come from the established churches, from one or more broadcasting organizations, and from donations and legacies.

The objections, however, cannot be overlooked – however exciting the dream. The balance of power between such a 'Church of the Air' and the institutional churches would be a delicate one. Who would really be responsible for what the electronic church did? – ultimately, I believe, the BBC and/or IBA, which act in such matters in consultation with the Central Religious Advisory Committee, on which the churches and other faiths are represented. There are, in fact, already examples of how broadcasting organizations and churches can work together to serve the public in certain of the existing Local Radio stations – for example BBC Radio Medway, which is an admirably ecumenical operation.

The trouble is, the more local the service becomes, the harder it is to break away from traditional 'churchianity' and get through to those who have rejected precisely that type of religion. The traditional parson or pious churchgoer is not necessarily a good broadcaster. 'Missioner of the Air' is a form of ministry the churches have yet to develop professionally, though there are training establishments which could undertake that and I have met a number of promising candidates.

There is a tension here between Independence and Ecumenism. In setting up a Church of the Air, would not the broadcasters be creating yet another church of their own? One for which they had no real mandate, public or divine? And what about the risk of personality cults developing, exploiting the media to wield immense spiritual, moral and maybe political power? And think of the openings for heresy!

Perhaps the most serious criticism is that it would really be *no* church. A voice on the air cannot supply community, cannot really tend a flock, nor (according to the most ancient doctrines of the Church) administer sacraments. It might lure people away from the true Church by offering a private and plastic substitute.

I have to acknowledge all these criticisms, and no one is more aware than I of the dangers and temptations facing the broadcaster who begins to collect a following in this field. 'Yours Faithfully' began as a journalistic commentary and has been drawn – by the demands of its audience – towards a deeper ministry. It is as if I had been invited into the pulpit to wire it for sound, and ended up conducting the service. In strictly journalistic terms, that is improper. But again, how can one ignore the appeal of those letters, telephone calls and personal approaches?

For me, the dilemma is unresolved. But the series 'Priestland's Progress' has led me into territory from which there is no turning back, though I should be glad of company and even competition. I have ventured to indicate where the journey is taking me by including, at the end of this collection, the text of a talk I gave as part of BBC Radio Medway's Lent Course in March 1982. I wish I could also have included a transcript of the stimulating ''phone-in' that followed, allowing some twenty listeners to make their points; for I am sure it is unhealthy for anyone in my privileged position not to be answered back.

I have learnt a great deal from my correspondence, some of it moving, some of it repellent. Most moving were the letters responding to my two talks on the suicide of Jacky Gillott, and those encouraging me to express what I saw as the Christian view of the Falklands crisis. By far the most repellent (apart from the obscene notes threatening to shoot the Pope) were those from animal-lovers bullying me to join the anti-field-sports campaign. 'Hip hip hip hooray for the God-given atom bomb!' snarled a gentleman from Malvern – oddly assuming that the bomb would kill all the nasty people and leave just the darling animals.

Still, I must thank all who have written to me. I must thank, also, the BBC for giving me the opportunity to write, broadcast and print these talks. My special gratitude is due to Colin Semper, David Winter, Rosemary Hartill and my other colleagues in the Religious Broadcasting Department for putting up with me; to my secretary, Pamela Almaz, whose sympathetic handling of my mail will be familiar to many listeners; to my wife Sylvia, without whose serenity I should have despaired long ago; to the music of J.S. Bach, and to the support of countless bishops, moderators, deans, canons, elders, prophets, depressives and rank-and-file children of God.

If it had not been more fitting to offer this, like previous volumes, To the Greater Glory of God, I should have dedicated it to the Unknown Believer.

GERALD PRIESTLAND

Bishops For All

28 June 1980

'I know I shall be called a wrecker,' said the Bishop of Truro, Dr Graham Leonard, 'but with deep regret I honestly have to say that I hope the Synod will reject this plan.'

Wreckers have a rather sinister reputation in Cornwall, but there is nothing predatory about Dr Leonard's attitude towards the Churches' Council for Covenanting and its plan to bring the Church oi England, the Methodists, United Reformed, Moravians and Churches of Christ to the threshold of unity. In a minority report which he and two other Anglican Catholics have appended to the scheme, the Bishop insists that integrity and loyalty to the truth and their mandate forbid their approval.

What is the Council proposing? The climax would be a giant service (probably in an open air stadium) at which the five churches, having individually ratified their Covenant together – would pledge that 'Within this covenant our communicant members will be welcomed without question at the Holy Communion in each of our churches; and that we recognize and accept one another's ministries as true ministries of word and sacrament in the holy catholic Church. We undertake to share a common ordinal in which bishops, presbyters and laity fulfil their proper service and to conduct all future ordinations in common. We also bind ourselves to develop methods of decision-making in common; and we undertake to respect the rights of conscience, consistent with the visible unity of the Church.' (I have slightly abbreviated the vows.) In keeping with this, the five churches would then act together by immediately ordaining at least one bishop and one minister, or 'presbyter', from each and celebrating the Lord's Supper together.

This would not in itself make a single United Church. But it would make less sense of a parish having two or three different ministers, each with a separate building, and it would make the logic of local mergers harder to resist. The Covenant is designed to clear two thorny hurdles: first, any suggestion that nonconformist ministers are not already valid, and need re-ordaining; and second, the acceptance of episcopacy by the nonconformists, which remains (in the eyes of the Anglican Catholics) the acid test – though they also maintain that theologically you cannot validate ministries by simply 'recognizing' them.

For the Methodists and Moravians, episcopacy has not been a major problem. But when you think what it has meant to the Congregationalists and Presbyterians of the United Reformed, you realize how much of a concession they have made. In a sense they have made it by acknowledging that their elected moderators are, in effect, bishops and may as well be *called* that if it will help; and that after the Covenant, all future moderators will be ordained bishops in one of these common services. But (and this is where the Anglican Catholics growl even louder) there will be a transitional period when not all URC moderators will have been so ordained. It may be seven years before the process works through.

To the Anglican Catholics this reveals a half-hearted, functional view of bishops which is out of keeping with the sacramental, historic and apostolic episcopacy which they see as essential to the Church of England's claim to be Catholic. They are not prepared to move closer to the nonconformists at the expense of moving away from the

Roman Catholics and the Orthodox – even if, it has to be said, there is far less likelihood of the Church of England uniting with *them* in the foreseeable future.

The awkward fact of women among the nonconformist ministry is another repellent to the High Church; and so is the prospect of all that voting, decision-making and conscientious objection. Not to mention a preliminary five years of Synodical debate and legislation.

It would be partisan to question the charity or sincerity of the Anglo-Catholics, and foolish to underestimate their chance of blocking the Covenant in the Synod. Shades of the Anglican-Methodist Scheme and of Women's Ordination hang heavy, and this year's Synod elections will be crucial. To some, the objections raised will seem reactionary and ungenerous – a refusal to let the Holy Spirit guide the Church into new paths. Others will remain baffled as to whom the Church thinks it is for.

Court's Critique

5 July 1980

Here comes Pornography; or rather, here comes Professor John Court, of South Australia, whose contention that pornography (far from being harmless) can be positively proved to do damage was given such a rough ride by the Williams Committee on Obscenity. The Professor, sponsored by Mrs Whitehouse's National Viewers and Listeners Association, is touring Britain to launch his new book *Pornography – A Christian Critique*. Its purpose, which is quite legitimate (and many will think wholesome) is to forestall any attempt to relax the restrictions on pornography in line with the Williams recommendations. Indeed the Professor would like to turn the tide the other way.

I am in no position to challenge or support his statistical arguments, with which he dismisses not only Williams but the 1970 report of the United States Presidential Commission. As with the many reports on Violence and Television, one has the weary feeling that sociology tends to reverse its findings every five years. But you don't have to use any of the statistics to agree in principle with most of Professor Court's final conclusions. He considers that pornography is against the family, against humanity, against women, against children, against culture, against God, even against sex itself in its deepest meanings. These judgements, I believe, are fair enough in the light of Christian moral values – indeed, of any religious values; for I can't see, either, that you need to rummage through the Bible to find support for them. All you really need to do is to break away from a totally solipsistic or selfish view of our purpose in the world – though of course Jews, Christians and many others would go a great deal further than that. To them, pornography (I do not say the erotic) is a kind of blasphemy because it degrades, exploits and desecrates that of God which is in everyone.

So what does Professor Court think we should do? No witch-hunting or book-burning he says. But churches could make a stand locally, and (I quote): 'Some Christians need to make it their special ministry to influence the media [and] to guide others to the appropriate response.' Again: 'We should not be ashamed to advocate censorship . . . Nevertheless, the very word generates a negative reaction [and] censorship alone cannot eliminate the problem.'

Professor Court then introduces the idea of what he calls 'Quality Control', claiming that in industry it is quite usual to insist upon a minimum standard with external controls. I think what he really means is 'Consumer Protection', which is fashionable enough, though what the standards would be and who the inspectors, he does not suggest. He closes by urging Christians to bear witness by the way they live and to back up politicians who work for what he calls 'restraints on pornography and for media responsibility in general'.

So the Professor is talking about discipline not just for blue films and dirty bookshops, but for publishing, broadcasting, theatres and cinemas 'in general'. Call it 'thin end of the wedge' if you will; or cry, 'High time, too!' I should not be surprised if we were to enter a period of media and artistic restraints. The feeling is in the air, I think, that things would improve all round if only the merchants of muck were made to observe some rules. But I should be surprised if the churches gained much satisfaction from it in the end, and if the result really were a return to beauty and truth.

The freedom of expression involved in pornography is a freedom of relatively little importance to the human spirit. Even John Stuart Mill granted there were exceptions to absolute liberty. Controls are not necessarily the works of the Devil, but virtuous folk need to be very careful whose controls they are, who is enforcing them, and why. They also need to know what is likely to be left after the purge: whether there really is healthy growth waiting to take the place of the weeds, or whether there will be nothing but a sterile wasteland. It is much easier to suppress what offends us, or to parrot dried-up formulas from the past, than to create something positive for our times.

Tradition! Tradition!

12 July 1980

I doubt if there will be much ballyhoo over those *other* elections taking place this autumn – not for the Presidency and Congress of the United States, but for the General Synod of the Church of England. Yet they deserve the closest possible attention, leading to the highest attainable poll, in view of their ability to make or break the Covenant for Unity with the Methodist and United Reformed churches. With its last gasp, the outgoing Synod voted to 'Take note' of the proposals – a noncommittal form of words which would not have killed the Covenant whichever way the vote went, though a *refusal* to Take Note would have gravely wounded it. As things turned out, it survives; but the complex arithmetic of Synod voting (which requires separate majorities among bishops, clergy and laity) would have made its final passage a toss-up in the outgoing assembly – and who-knows-what in the Synod yet to come. Hence the importance of the elections, which ought to concentrate the minds of every diocese in the land.

As reported in an earlier note in this series, the Covenant was commended by six out of the nine Anglicans who helped to draft it. The other three – Anglican Catholics, headed by the Bishop of Truro – advised Synod to reject it. Their reasons were developed in the Synod's debate. Mr Maurice Chandler emphasized the expense and the interminable legislation that would be involved. Mr John Gummer was accused of arrogance for adumbrating that there was no longer any good reason for being anything *but* an Anglican or a Catholic. But the two main issues that emerged were our old friends Episcopacy and the Ordination of Women.

The Covenant provides for the bishoping of United Reformed Moderators – though any who are in office at the time of the Covenant may remain as they are until they retire; and the Anglican Catholics have seen this as a demonstration that the United Reformed are not sincerely accepting the historic and apostolic episcopacy in its true and sacramental sense. Sacramental is a very important word, but almost impossible to explain to those who don't normally use it. I always annoy somebody when I say that it conveys a certain Holy Magic, but it's the best quick way I can think of. It may perhaps help you to understand Canon Peter Boulton (one of the High Church Three) when he says: 'The action of accepting quasi-episcopal persons as though they were bishops is tantamount to an admission that in the last resort, bishops are an administrative convenience. We do not believe the Church of England can or should play with the episcopate as if it were a privately-owned treasure that we can dispense to others in larger or smaller doses. It is a gift of God which we have received as part of our membership of the Church Catholic.' Well, that is what I meant by Holy Magic, and obviously it is *not* the same as saying 'Moderators are overseers, just like bishops'.

Thirty-five Anglican bishops against two were prepared to Take Note; and some of them went a good deal further. The Bishop of Birmingham said that the Church of England was being asked whether its present romantic and unrealistic love affair with Rome was so obsessive that it was prepared to turn itself into a sect. The Church had expected great things under Archbishop Runcie's primacy, but if this final initiative was turned down, we couldn't hope for much. (The Archbishop remained silent throughout.) The Bishop of Durham identified 'unconscious Anglican Imperialism'. The Bishop of St Albans feared the Church of England would lose credibility in the eyes of her sister churches. The Bishop of Winchester declared, 'I believe in the God of Movement and Growth, not in the God of the Cut and Dried.' And the Bishop of Guildford told those who insisted that Truth was in the Episcopacy: 'Truth is in the Living God – nowhere else.'

That was a rare moment of passion – something lacking in a debate of largely set speeches. Synod congratulated itself on being so well-mannered. And yet, with so much at stake, *was* that so admirable? Let us hope that the new Synod will be both thoroughly representative and prepared to say what it really feels.

In Hubbard's Cupboard

19 July 1980

After a dozen years, the ban on missionaries of the Scientology Church entering Britain has been lifted. It was imposed in 1968 by the Secretary for Health, on the grounds that Scientology was 'a socially harmful pseudo-philosophical cult'. Its removal was recommended in 1971, following the enquiry by Sir John Foster, QC, and a good deal of parliamentary sympathy has built up over the years since. To ban a religion is, on the face of it, contrary to the traditions of the land. It would be hard to justify before the courts of the European Community, and anyway is difficult to enforce. And so the ban is to go; though it should be noted that individuals whose presence is deemed not conducive to the public good may still be excluded by the immigration Rules.

And why should Scientology be discriminated against when all kinds of Moonies, gurus and oriental meditationists can dance in our streets and hold seminars in our country houses? Can the explanation be that Scientology is not a religion at all, but a dangerous form of amateur tinkering with the mind? – and a lucrative one, at that, for the hierarchy of the movement. There is little doubt in my mind that such a suspicion lay behind the ban. Can it, on the other hand, be that the opposition was sponsored by a sinister alliance of established Medical and Defence interests who themselves were involved in tinkering with the nervous system and were fearful of being unmasked by Scientology? There you have the cases behind the cases.

I have before me the official Background and Ceremonies of the Church of Scientology, copyright to the founder Mr L. Ron Hubbard, a golden cross upon its cover. Described as 'a non-denominational applied religious philosophy', Scientology claims descent from Vedic Hinduism, through Buddhism and the Gospel of St John – with a bow to the Quakers – on to Mr Hubbard himself. Mr Hubbard disparages Forgiveness, saying a truly great person loves his fellows because he understands them – 'Never desire revenge', he says, though he includes a coldly vindictive reference to what I take to be one or other of the assassinated Kennedy brothers.

Later we find The Creed. It includes such statements as, 'We of the Church believe – That all men have inalienable rights to their sanity . . . That the study of the mind and the healing of mentally-caused ills should not be alienated from religion or condoned in non-religious fields . . . That man is basically good . . . That the spirit alone may save or heal the body.' Well, there are superficial points in common here with Christian Science. But the argument is that man will be saved by his own efforts, and not by the grace of Christ.

Indeed, it is very hard to find Christ in Scientology, and I doubt if any mainstream Christian – or Jew, Sikh or Muslim – would accept it as religious at all. In general, one gets the impression of a form of woolly Humanism, much concerned with mental health and bitter towards orthodox medical practice. The key may lie in Mr Hubbard's own life; for the official biography tells us that he once astounded his doctors by curing himself of blindness and other disabilities, through the recognition that (I quote): 'The mind can change the body, but the body only slightly alters the mind.' And so he developed what he calls 'Dianetics – the Modern Science of Mental Health'. In a nutshell, it is a form of 'talking out' psychotherapy, guided by a kind of lie detector.

For more than twenty years the Scientologists have attracted the unfavourable attentions of the United States Government, on grounds of practising quack medicine, tax-dodging and general subversion. The latter suspicion has been encouraged by the Scientologists' diligence in digging up and disseminating any sort of evidence to support their contention that medicine and psychiatry (in Britain as well as the United States) have been perverted in the service of dirty tricks like germ warfare and mind control. Indeed, dirty tricks have been alleged on both sides.

Well, sniping at modern medicine and psychiatry is as easy as throwing stones at a cow – you can hardly miss. But even if the cow is sacred, doubts must remain whether it is a religious or philosophical activity. Nor does being persecuted – or prosecuted – certify the victim as necessarily righteous.

Theology by the Foot

26 July 1980

The silly season is upon us – in religion as elsewhere: everybody is straining for the release of a holiday from the intense seriousness with which everything has to be treated these days, longing for the chance to get away to some quiet beach and shout 'Nonsense! Rubbish! It's all a load of old toffee paper!' But, sorry, not everybody, after all. For I seem to be getting more and more letters and pamphlets from people who have seen the light in the more obscure corners of the Bible and are determined to alert us all to the profound significance of their discoveries.

For example, something called The Rapture Preparation Crusade – in a series of Messages to the People of Britain – has been having visions of the most appalling kind, and wants us seriously to consider such passages as 'Except thou repent, I will come and remove thy candlestick'. One should not treat such warnings lightly, for an accompanying prophecy declares: 'You who rock with laughter in your offices when you hear My Word, even you shall be the first to rock with convulsions of inner pain and torment, for my angel shall descend first upon you.'

Since it is the silly season, let me for once tell you a fable.

Once in Northamptonshire – some time in the mid-seventeenth century – there lived the son of a cobbler, Judah Jones. Jones was a pious young man, after the manner of those days, and a great reader of his Bible. One day (and we are not sure whether he was reading Isaiah 52, Nahum 1 or Romans 10) there seemed to rise up from the page, in letters of gold, the words 'How beautiful upon the mountains are the *feet*'. Jones rushed out to find a mountain – not too easy in Northamptonshire – but his eye lit upon a local promontory known as Haggler's Hill, whither he bent his eager way. Arrived at the top, he saw a cloud with a pair of immense and beautiful feet emerging from it. And there came a voice proclaiming: 'Put off thy shoes from off thy feet!' Which he did, and the voice taught him, saying: 'The sceptre shall not depart from Judah, nor a lawgiver from between his feet. Surely the land whereon thy feet have trodden shall be thine inheritance. I will not suffer thy foot to be moved. I will keep the feet of my saints so that they swell not . . .' And so, indeed, it came to pass. Judah Jones became the celebrated barefoot apostle and one of his earliest converts was a local widow who married him and endowed him with Haggler's Hill and nine hundred acres. Thanks to his practice of walking barefoot throughout the land, Jones became the founder of the Natural Feet Movement – but there was more to it than that. He soon discovered (thanks to the Oxford Concordance to the Holy Scriptures) that there are approximately one hundred references to feet in the Bible, and that the theology and liturgy which could be developed from them were both moving and profound.

Central to the practice of Footism was the Double Lavation (as it came to be known): first a woman member of the congregation would anoint the minister's feet, drying them with her hair; then the minister would humbly wash the feet of all present. In the early days, much scandal and persecution arose from the efforts of Footites to attend the parish church unshod; and even greater scandal and trials for blasphemy when they built churches of their own containing a pair of white marble feet. Yet is has to be admitted that there is a certain charm in their contention that all Man can hope to see of his God are His Feet – which alone touch the Earth, and bring the message of Peace.

Today, of course, we know the Footites for their Free Clinics, which have spread world-wide; and for the young evangelists with towels and bowls of water, offering to wash feet in Oxford Street. Inevitably there have been schisms, notably between the Primitive Barefeet and those who adopted lightweight sandals – quoting John the Baptist as evidence that Our Lord himself wore them. They really are admirable people who illuminate a neglected aspect of our Faith – though perhaps their theology is a little obsessive, a trifle incomplete. They overlook Peter's prayer: 'Lord, not my feet only, but also my hands and my head.'

The Invisible Gardener

2 August 1980

'When', asked a friend of mine, 'are you going to tackle the one question on which your entire job depends – namely: Does God Exist?' And this particular friend, who doesn't believe in God and manages to lead as happy and valuable a life as I do, quoted to me the ambiguous fable of the garden.

When two men step into a garden, the first one looks about him and says: 'There is order and purpose here. I see in this the hand of a benevolent gardener, who comes in the night and tends the trees and flowers. Without him, none of this would be possible.' But the second man, surveying the same garden, declares: 'I see neither order nor purpose, though it is all pleasant enough. I know the natural laws which govern the growth and decay of the garden, but they do not require the presence of a gardener and I see no evidence of his existence. But, if you like, we will watch for him tonight.' And so they wait until dawn and see nobody. 'It does not surprise me,' says the first man, 'I should have told you, the gardener is invisible.'

The garden, of course, is the world, and some of us might say that if there is an invisible gardener, he is not much good at his job. However, believers and unbelievers might agree that, however the garden got planted, it is up to *us* to look after it – that we should not expect some invisible force to do our dirty work for us. Like any metaphor for the transcendent, that of the gardener is of strictly limited use.

I hope this discussion will not upset the people who write to me saying: 'Of *course* there is a God! The Bible says so, and describes him precisely, and it is wicked and subversive to raise the question!' But the fact is, even the greatest saints have experienced their moments of doubt and desertion, and there are plenty of good, honest people whose faith is hope rather than certainty, or who would like to believe but cannot. Millions, I dare say, are eager to have the existence of God proved to them. But I don't know a single logical proof of God that can't be knocked down. Too much depends on definitions. Nor is it much good trying to prove the existence of God scientifically; for science is always changing its mind, and in any case the God we are talking about is more than the laws of science – just as he is more than miraculous interventions *against* the laws of science. Impenetrable by logic, indefinable by science, the nearest we can get to him is through poetry or music – vague and approximate media which it is all too easy to dismiss as fantasy. At the risk of seeming to invoke his Invisibility: God is Love, and that is something you cannot measure or take apart – you can only experience it.

But what if you do not have the experience (a tough one, that); or if you decide that the experience is not God but physical, psychological or aesthetic well-being? But no, the

Sense of God is more than that, and can involve acute discomfort. The direct mystical *knowing* of God is far more common than used to be thought. But for many people it is the discovery that faith – that simply believing in God – *works*, that is the real proof. Ah, says the sceptic, of course it does. Nobody who has committed himself to the nonsense 'I believe in the invisible and unprovable' is going to admit he's wrong. But it wouldn't be only he that was wrong: it would have been ninety-nine per cent of mankind, for the existence of Deity has always been part of us. Whether you worship a stone on the moors or the Trinity in St Peter's, the I-and-Thou relationship is there. No reason, you may say, why we shouldn't grow out of it, just as we have stopped believing in the Flat Earth, fairies and magic spells. But I suggest the Sense of God is of a quite different order from those – that it is a characteristic of the human species, perhaps our most important, though it can atrophy if it is not exercised. Troubles come when we try to express our apprehensions of the infinite in finite language, like the metaphor of the garden.

For most of my listeners (most of the time) it is just plain silly to ask whether God exists – let alone try to answer it in four minutes. We don't just believe – we know. But we don't know in the way that we know a gardener exists, because God is more than a cosmic gardener. Just what he is, what he's up to, how we can know him better, takes more than one lifetime to find out.

Holy Hackwork

9 August 1980

There is in Britain, unnoticed by most addicts of Fleet Street, a considerable underworld press – the religious press. Economically it's nonsense, journalistically amateur, yet people are always trying to start new papers, convinced that somewhere out there are thousands of Christian readers yearning to read Christian truth prepared by Christian writers. On the other hand, one of the most lively religious papers we have is the *Jewish Chronicle*, which has a bigger circulation than the *Church Times* and is much, much louder. The notion of keeping religion and politics apart is incomprehensible to my Jewish friends, but the *Chronicle* does illustrate one of the essential functions of the religious press – to bind a community together by keeping up communications within it. At the other end of the spectrum is a quiet grey paper called *The Friend*, the weekly mag. of the Quakers; but it serves precisely that purpose, and without it the Quakers would probably fade away. Its editorial is always a gem.

The temptation for any religious paper is to become a kind of private whistling in the dark. It has to ask itself, is it trying to speak outwards and serve the world – or inwards to a limited community? A prime example of the outward-looking is the *Christian Science Monitor*, which is a good paper by any secular standard, as well as a credit to its church. On the other hand, you find some evangelical papers which profess to be speaking to the world, but do it in a language only intelligible to the converted.

Booming away at the top of the religious circulation is

undoubtedly the Roman Catholic tabloid weekly *The Universe*, with its almost compulsory photo of the Pope (or at least the Cardinal) on the front. It's a clean, private, predigested family paper, and rather too easy to make fun of. I shall always treasure the kiddies' corner saying: 'Remember, children, Robin Hood, Maid Marian, and their Merry Men *were Catholics*.'

I've never quite understood why the rival paper, *The Catholic Herald*, which has less than a quarter of the *Universe* circulation, doesn't do better. It hasn't the cosiness, I suppose, and its front page news must sometimes alarm the faithful. But it has a superb cartoonist in John Ryan, and the sublime Patrick O'Donovan writing on the back. Come to that, a Catholic weekly – *The Tablet* – is consistently better value than the *New Statesman* or *Spectator*, and without the priestliness of some of the Catholic monthlies. But here we are getting into theologically deeper water.

What should the layman read who takes his religion seriously and wants to dabble in a little light theology? There is no substitute at all for the *Church Times* – for its regular columnists, its reviews, its correspondence page and its news – for it even gets scoops; no amateur journalism here. The *Church Times* used to have a reputation for being unfair to evangelicals, but I can't see that today; nor is there any alternative with half so broad a mind. Frankly, it is indispensable.

One day I hope I shall be able to say the same of *Theology*, the SPCK-based review which is now claiming some modest success in breaking out of the dog-collar towards a more general readership. It is very nicely printed and reviews my own books most generously, but it is maddening on two counts: first, it comes out every *other* month (making it a hard habit to acquire), and its book reviews can be over a year late. Partly printers' time-lag – partly that you can't crack a whip over your contributors if you aren't paying them anything . . .

And there's the rub. If religious editors could pay more, they could command better work and offer a more professional paper to a wider public. But how to raise the money from a readership which may be impoverished, but is often downright stingy and would sooner borrow than buy? So ignore my prejudices, but do buy a religious paper if you possibly can: you will be helping to build up an alternative press (for example, the *Methodist Recorder* might become the journal of Christian conscience it shows signs of trying to be); you will help your church to know about itself; and you might even help a few downtrodden holy hacks to make a relatively honest living.

Nothing Inflammatory

16 August 1980

When he took office, Archbishop Runcie promised to think before he spoke. The other day he gave a good example of that. In a carefully checked and measured statement (on which the media were wisely not invited to press him) he insisted that neither Miss Jean Waddell nor Dr John Coleman and his wife had been dabbling in Iranian politics, nor were they anything but servants of the Iranian Church. All that was clearly for the ears of the Ayatollah Khomeini. But the Archbishop concluded with some words for the rest of us: 'There is an inevitable danger', he said, 'that understandable frustration about the situation will lead to inflammatory statements; but I hope that nothing will be done to upset the wise and sober attempts being made to ensure that Jean Waddell and her friends come home safely.' In other words, if we really are more interested in getting these people out of danger than in letting off useless steam, we should resist the temptation to curse Islam and take it out on the Iranian students.

The Archbishop's advice has a significance even beyond the collision with the Ayatollah. One gets the impression that the world is now full of yelling demonstrators. The urge is irresistible to cry: 'Law and Order! Get them off the streets!' – which is what the Shah did, and look where it got him. Quite apart from any tradition of free speech and assembly, caring for our neighbour involves listening to him, even if we don't like what he's saying. We take the rightness of our own views for granted – and if we're lucky, they're assumed in the media; but when somebody has something new or unorthodox to say, something which may be half batty but has instructive elements in it too, then he finds it very difficult to get a hearing. What else can he do but shout? And so he ends up as a rabble-rouser and 'demonstrator'. Which is not to say that everything he stands for is true. But if we all shout, and nobody listens, we can only end up hitting each other: precisely what Christians are forbidden to do.

Alas, the chances of the Ayatollah listening to the Archbishop are slender. When the Ayatollah received an envoy of the Pope recently, the envoy was brusquely told that mission schools were 'nests of spies', Catholic priests agents of the West, and that the Pope would be better employed protesting about Iranian students being tortured by the Americans. To dismiss that as pure malice is to overlook several points which it is in our own interests to understand. The first is that behind the Iranian Revolution lie generations of humiliated nationalists and a resentment of foreign domination which is not wholly without cause.

Islam has become the vehicle for that resentment, for it alone is seen as native to Iran. International churches like the Roman and Anglican, with their foreign contacts, letters and travels abroad, are caught up in this despite Dr Runcie's denials. Spies and agents *do* exist (the American hostage rescue attempt depended on them); but often the words are extended to mean anyone who is held responsible for misinforming the outside world about the Revolution – and Iranians are acutely aware of not being understood as they would wish.

They don't, of course, help us much. Iranian Jews have been disgracefully treated, because Jews equal Israel. Any church in touch with Jerusalem falls under the same suspicion. Others have been punished for having co-educational schools or using communion wine – contrary to Islamic teaching. The hostility goes a long way back, for the Koran itself contains some invincible misunderstandings: the Prophet, for example, was totally incapable of seeing the point of the Trinity or the Crucifixion. 'They worship their rabbis and their monks', thunders the Koran, 'and the Messiah the son of Mary, as gods beside Allah; though they were ordered to serve one God only!'

The Iranian revolutionaries see only the black side of us, as we see only the black side of them. It is tempting to conclude that there is nothing for it but to hit back – which is fine if you actually want a war. Otherwise there is really no alternative to patience, a certain detachment, and an effort to show that Christendom has values of sacrifice and forgiveness by which it lives. Like, for example, those of the Colemans and Jean Waddell.

Easter People

23 August 1980

'We are an Easter People, and Alleluia is our song!' cried John Paul II. 'Alleluia indeed', sighed Archbishop Worlock of Liverpool, surveying with relief the forty-thousand-word booklet *The Easter People*, summing up the reactions of the Roman Catholic hierarchy to the National Pastoral Congress of last May. It had been a hard slog.

At first sight – and maybe second – the document resembles a large soft loaf without any crunch to it and a good deal of aeration. The bishops insist it is not their 'response' to the Congress – which is an indication of the subtlety which repeated mastication reveals. Many people assume the Church of Rome operates from a set of rigid and immutable doctrines; and it often encourages that belief. It shudders at words like 'rescind', 'revision' or 'change'. But 'development' is another matter, for it suggests the growth of shoots already there on the existing branch. It is fascinating to watch Catholic theologians searching a document for shoots that might be coaxed into growth; and the subtlety with which Catholic doctrine is written often renders that possible – *This* can be interpreted in the light of *That*, fresh 'insights' can be gained into the essential meaning of *The Other*. The cynic might call it opportunism, casuistry; but it would be more charitable to recognize the Church's duty not to be carried away overnight by the variable winds of change – quite apart from the sheer theological difficulty (some would say impossibility) of admitting a mistake. For the Church, a U-turn takes a long time – so long, it may be barely perceptible.

It is possible to go through *The Easter People* noting a series of apparent negatives: no artificial birth-control, no women priests, married priests, Communion for the divorced, shared Communion with non-Catholics and so forth. But again, that is to miss the subtleties. The reports that went up to the bishops from the Congress had their subtleties too. The section dealing with marriage and family life did *not* say: 'Legalize contraception, and who cares if the kids make love!' Tactfully they distinguished contraception from abortion, stressed that they were concerned with responsible married couples, and called for a fundamental re-examination of the Church's teaching in the comprehensive area of marriage, sexuality and contraception. They urged the Church to listen to the experience of married people as to the meaning of sexual relations.

It's important, I think, to note how deeply concerned the Congress and the bishops were for the old-fashioned, abused and battered family – and it's good to know that somebody is. The bishops were grateful for what they called this sensitive and constructive approach from the direction of marriage rather than that of isolated sex. They reaffirmed the encyclical *Humanae Vitae* which, constitutionally, they were in no position to deny. But (and here lie the shoots of 'development') they admitted the Church had not completely worked out its understanding of marriage, though it was on the move. It must take account of sex not just as an act of procreation but 'as a communication of love and self . . . in which a couple affirm each other's identity . . . heal and sustain each other and . . . make Christ sacramentally present to each other'. If the sexual act is now to be emphasized as the ultimate personal communication, a spiritual experience, a sacrament, then openness to conception begins to look a rather less important issue.

Behind this lies the readiness of Archbishop Worlock

and his colleagues – despite the pressures upon them of the Magisterium – to listen to their people and acknowledge the need for 'development'. And there are other examples, among them the question of married men as priests, and of Holy Communion for the divorced. There is one other concern which may, I think, produce some surprises – the concern for more adult education in the faith, on the grounds that much of the discontent among the laity arises from failure to understand the Church's teachings. That may be so. On the other hand, more study, more understanding can lead to more criticism and to more demands for change. Applause for *The Easter People* will be widespread, but it won't be unanimous.

For the Price of One

30 August 1980

Having minded the shop through August, I'll be off on my late summer hols next month; and before I go, there are a couple of points I'd like to leave with you, so this week you get two for the price of one.

The first arises from the *Guardian* newspaper's amusing pursuit of Mrs Thatcher's mole-catcher, the Mr Bingham of Epsom who is supposed to be plugging the leaks in Whitehall and got leaked himself. By chance, one of the *Guardian*'s own men, David Leigh, has just put out an extremely lucid book called *The Frontiers of Secrecy*, pointing out the hollowness of our claim to be a government of the people, by the people, for the people. On the contrary, he argues, we are governed by our betters (or those who think they are) and the last thing they want is troublesome, ignorant 'people' peering over their shoulders and reading their interdepartmental memos.

Now it seems to me that private persons are entitled to privacy; and that if you are manoeuvring against a clearly defined enemy – be he criminal or spy or terrorist – you may even be entitled to secrecy. But is there any guidance in morals or religion for the conduct of public affairs in private? One would have thought that the Christian tradition was one of openness: it may be going a bit far to insist that the affairs of the United Kingdom be conducted like a tribal meeting of the Children of Israel, but surely the commandment against bearing false witness does cover dissembling, and surely also there is a permanent injunction to the mighty to remember the humble and meek (the people) and not to imagine that the whole show is for their benefit. If there is a Christian theology of government its emphasis lies on *service*, not *power*.

On the other hand it would, I think, be unChristian to assume that our rulers aspire to tyranny. Like the rest of us they are trying to cope with the impossible, trying to please the Boss, trying to avoid that dread of every office: TROUBLE. Rather than suspicion, perhaps we should feel sorry for them – sorry that they haven't the confidence and trust in God and their fellow men to be open. Openness frees; secrecy enslaves.

As you see, I've been reading the papers: for the next thing to catch my eye was a pair of letters to *The Times* expressing astonishment at what the Roman Catholic bishops said last week about married love being (I quote): 'A relationship in which a couple affirm each other's identity . . . and through which they make Christ sacramentally present to each other.' To some commentators that sounded like a delicate attempt to develop a path round the Church's ban on artificial contraception; but the two letter writers chose to gag at the gobbledygook. What on earth, they asked, was such jargon doing masquerading as the Word of God?

I don't know why a churchman should object to a spot of jargon. Is it really more difficult to accept terms like 'affirming identity' and 'making Christ sacramentally present' than it is to accept that marriage (which is not held to be complete until consummation) 'signifies the mystical union that is betwixt Christ and his Church'? I wonder how many couples have walked down the aisle believing *that's* what they were doing. (If they did, of course, that would only confirm the sacramental presence.) But I fancy the real objection is to bringing Christ into the sex act and suggesting it could be in any sense a presentation of holiness.

Why not, though? The claim seems to me to be verified by experience. I know the statement 'God is Love' doesn't baldly mean 'God is Sex', and that two people can express love without sex. But unless we are going to stick with St Augustine's anti-human animal view of sex, why should it be offensive to say that the act of love is a communion of the deepest in two people, that of God in each of them? Or should the commandment 'Love one another' have been followed by the postscript 'But not by *making* love to one another'? Not only is there the healing and support of which the bishops speak, there is also that mutual affirmation of identity – 'I acknowledge you as uniquely you, and us as uniquely one.'

Nor is this an upstart theology. Pius XI in 1930, and Vatican II some thirty years later, both got the point that marital union was not just a matter of begetting children or else taking sinful pleasure. In its completeness the sacrament of marriage is indivisible, not part sacred, part profane.

Valley of Shadow

4 October 1980

For me the joy of life has been clouded by the recent death of a good friend and fellow broadcaster, Jacky Gillott. As you probably heard, she took her own life while suffering from Depression. May she rest in peace.

I don't want to make this too personal, and when I say that in addition to her skills, her intelligence and her beauty she was admired without jealousy, I am only trying to establish that here was someone who apparently had everything going for her – and yet killed herself. Goodness knows she worked hard enough, perhaps too hard, but we are not paid to tell the public what agony it can be serving it: what is seen and heard often appears to be effortless success. And the successful must surely be happy – they may even *look* happy. But, oh no, they aren't, and money is no help. As Mary Kenny wrote last Sunday: 'The glittering prizes mean nothing in the end.' And so there is a long list of successful, loved and admired people who did not love or admire themselves – who loathed themselves so much that, in the end, they destroyed themselves. I don't believe this is a purely modern phenomenon – English history and literature are full of such cases, though perhaps the means of destruction are more temptingly available now.

So Jacky Gillott was one of many; and on behalf of others confronting that valley of shadow I would like to appeal for understanding. I think I am entitled to, for I have been there myself and, I hope, come through it.

Depression, with a big D, has little to do with the perfectly normal experience of 'feeling a bit depressed' about something specific; it doesn't necessarily have anything to do with being tired or in poor physical health, either. And it is an illness, not a madness. There are several varieties, but as I know it, Depression is like a dark mist lurking in the corners of the room, always there, always ready to come surging forward and rising up to envelop you. It is blackness, it is emptiness, it is meaninglessness and total inner despair. Others may think you are fortunate, but *you* know it is all an empty fraud, and that one day the hollow balloon will burst, you will be found out and your crime exposed. What crime? You don't know; you only know you are guilty; and you can hear them coming down the corridor to get you. The penalty, of course, is death and you might as well be your own executioner.

Two things give you pause: how to do it, and the sorrow it will bring to those you love; though actually you know you are so worthless they'll soon get over it and be better off without you. You also know that nobody will believe you are the criminal, the fraud, you know yourself to be – and so you tell no one. Which is why everyone is so staggered when one of these fortunate, successful people commits suicide. I worked on the same programme as Jacky for months – and neither of us recognized the Depression of the other.

As I say, cases vary. Many of us are saved. *I* say Thank God for modern drugs and psychiatry. Though I have read books and heard of cases where Depression was healed by Faith, I can't personally recommend it. For me, Religion only increased the sense of worthlessness and guilt; illness deepened the chasm between myself and God; a sick mind could only conceive a sickened religion. *My* conversion experience was on the psychiatrist's couch. Once the drift towards annihilation had been halted by some rather nasty little pills, once the skeletons had been dragged from their cupboards and given decent burial, only then could Love resume its health and primacy. I wish I could say that Christian Faith gives immunity to Depression, but I know too many cases where it didn't.

That in itself may sound depressing, but it should turn us towards practical measures. Symptoms like early waking and professions of worthlessness need to be taken very seriously. If this has been a gloomy talk, I apologize: there is hope, there are more rescues than drownings. But to see a fellow swimmer go under at last still makes one groan, 'Why, Lord? Why?'

The Grey Fellowship

18 October 1980

A fortnight ago I devoted this talk to some thoughts on the death of my friend and fellow broadcaster, Jacky Gillott, who took her own life while suffering from Depression. The response has quite overwhelmed my resources. Something like four hundred letters came in, all worth reading and indeed every one of them read. It has been a very humbling privilege to receive so many confidences. The grey fellowship of the depressed is wider than it knows, and the sad thing is that so many of its members should turn to a total stranger rather than to their doctors, ministers or families. I am afraid the point has now been reached, however, where I must close down my amateur clinic and use today's talk to answer the unanswered. I hope they will excuse me.

Let me summarize what I said before. I began by recording the fact – too easily forgotten – that successful people are not necessarily happy people – that there is a long list of loved and admired figures who did not love or admire themselves – who loathed themselves so much that in the end they killed themselves. And then I attempted, from my own experience, to give some idea of what it is like to suffer the curse of Depression – the blackness, emptiness and total despair. Whatever others may think, you know you are worthless and that one day your crime will be unmasked – a crime which you do not even know, but for which the penalty is death. And because nobody will believe this, you can tell nobody. Underneath is a terrible violence.

And I went on to say that although I had heard of cases where faith was the healer, in my own experience (and that of many others) religion only increased the sense of guilt. Personally I thanked God for the gift of modern drugs and psychiatry and their renewal of faith.

As I say, the response was overwhelming. Depression takes several forms but well over half my letters said: 'That is how it was with me' – *was* because most of those writers had been helped through it. There *are* more rescues than drownings. And it was good to hear from so many doctors and priests saying 'We *do* understand – we *can* help'. A London psychiatrist wrote: 'Current orthodox treatments may not be perfect, but we do not have better.' For what my judgement is worth, I believe that. If I could get one message through to the grey fellowship, it would be: *Let* your doctor, *let* your family help you. You cannot just 'pull yourself together', but when help is offered, trust it and meet it half way.

When help is offered . . . There were perhaps a dozen letters which boldly declared: the only help you need is faith in God – and you, Mr Priestland, have betrayed him by suggesting otherwise. Not more than a couple of these letters actually came from depressives; and one very unpleasant one, from Torquay, outlined the final extermination at the hands of Satan awaiting the self-murderer. Well, I do not know if I am expected to be dishonest for Christ, but I was speaking from my own doubtless unworthy experience; and I can quote from one of my letters that says: 'I too, nun that I am, have been down into the pit, and consider it to have been the most revealing experience of my human weakness. You ended your talk "Why, Lord, why?" and I wanted to shout "Look at a crucifix".'

Well, while in Depression, I found that unbearable. Now I think I hear the words 'My God, my God, why hast Thou forsaken me? . . . and on the third day, he rose again'. Lucky are those who are spared their crucifixion. Those who are not spared it share a great mystery.

As I say, there are those willing to help the victim down from his or her cross, though alas not enough of them, not always with success. But make no mistake, Depression is a disease that kills, and we should be on the lookout for it among those we love – including ourselves, for a lack of self-love is one of the most dangerous symptoms. I hope this does not start a rush to the surgeries – just a spot of glumness does not count – but if Jacky Gillott's sufferings on her own personal cross can lead to the resurrection of only a few others, then her sufferings – and the sufferings of many who have written to me – will not be in vain.

The Crucible

25 October 1980

Some time back I took a quick look round the ecclesiastical press: and promptly got scolded for the ones I didn't mention. Rightly I was ticked off for not mentioning the

Salvation Army's mass circulation *War Cry* (which has just come out with a splendid front page in defence of being unashamedly old-fashioned). Rightly I was reproached for not drawing attention to the Church of Ireland's *Gazette* (with its admirable columnist Cromlyn) and the Church of Scotland's *Life and Work*. And rightly reminded of that great family of Parish, Deanery and Diocesan magazines, ranging from the brilliant to the deplorable. It's a matter of space as well as taste; but whatever your taste may be, my underlying message remains: do support your church paper. You wouldn't want it to go the way of *The Times*, and shut down, would you?

Today I want to give special mention to one I left out before, because I think this month's issue of *Crucible* – the quarterly journal of the Church of England's Board for Social Responsibility – deserves it. *Crucible* costs 75 pence a time, is well turned out, lucidly written and offers relentless proof of how, why and where the Church belongs in the world of politics, economics and social relations.

Its editorial this time is quite stern about this, however: 'God's first concern is with the poor' (it says), 'and there is a Word to be spoken on that theme to the British people and their government . . . But a Word which is nothing but words will not be heard.' In short, the editorial is asking the Church just how it proposes the money be found for bigger Child Benefits.

Next an article by John Sleeman which might have been subtitled 'The Bible and Thatcherism' (or to be precise, 'An Economico-Theological Critique of the Radical Right'), out of which the Radical Right does not come too well in Mr Sleeman's eyes.

However, it's the Church that gets put in its place in the following essay, on Industrial Relations, by Keith Archer. (Quite incidentally, this opened my eyes to the meaning of the word Crisis – in Greek – not as a dangerous moment of decision but as a judgement, God's judgement, a consequence.) However, the real point of Mr Archer's essay is that the Church should be more humble in looking for and recognizing Secular Grace. After studying various strikes, he finds that it's not just the Gospel which can illuminate the secular; it can very well happen the other way round.

Then Canon John Austin Baker on Racism and the Bible: not by any means just another lecture about how unChristian it is to hate blacks, for it starts off by declaring that the Bible says nothing about racism for the simple reason that the Ancient World never knew the idea. The Roman Empire, for example, had many other vicious obsessions, but it was a genuinely multi-racial society. Canon Baker goes on to point out that biologically there are no different races of humanity; he then faces up squarely to the awkward fact of IQ differences and to the anti-Jewish propaganda in the New Testament. Certainly he arrives at the conclusion that for Christians the only race is the human race, but Christians don't win any prizes on the way.

The final article in *Crucible* is by Michael Hare-Duke, Bishop of St Andrews, on 'The External Pressures on Marriage'; and I would have thought it was just the thing for those middle-class Christian parents who are uncomfortably aware that their children are living – and loving – with a member of the opposite sex, happily and even faithfully, but don't seem to be getting married. I suppose some will find the Bishop trendy and permissive: he says things like 'Marriage was made for man and not man for marriage', or 'Husband and wife need not be trapped by marriage', or 'Living together can represent such a high view of marriage that a young person holds back from it, treating it as a serious relationship requiring a proper apprenticeship'. None the less, the Gospel is firmly there in the article and I think it may reassure a lot of parents suffering from an unnatural conflict of heart and conscience. What with Marriage, Thatcherism, Racism and Strikes, *Crucible* has a lot in its melting-pot this month.

Parting Shots

1 November 1980

This talk is not so much a note as a notebook. For tomorrow I'm off to India until the New Year, and I want to clear my desk before I go. What? Off again? Call it a sentimental pilgrimage from which I hope to return with some insight into what God has to say in a context utterly different from ours, a culture which is fully mature, which has admitted the Cross, but has not been converted to it. India has great spiritual strength – as I know from having lived there before – but what is it? I won't be so arrogant as to promise you the answer; but I'll try.

In the meantime, Rosemary Hartill will be minding the shop, and I can promise you excellent service. Among the goods on show will be, I suppose, a little more about the outcome of the recent Synod in Rome. It was hardly a breakthrough for pragmatism, but then if you've painted yourself into a corner it's hard to get out without leaving messy footmarks all over the place. What exasperates me is the Vatican's insistence upon non-communication. You'd think they'd been discussing defence secrets. But there speaks a nosy journalist.

There'll be a big sales drive for the new Alternative Service Book, and I dare say a good deal of sniping and blasting at it when it's published later this month. I must say, for myself, that I think the Church of England would have been remiss not to have produced it. Were I a vicar (which I am not – and not even qualified to be) I would vote for the ASB, study the New English Bible, and use the Book of Common Prayer and King James. But it's one of the glories of the Church of England that such behaviour would be perfectly legal, and long may it continue.

Two very worthwhile documents have fallen upon my desk this week, and I commend them to you. One is a commentary upon the three major reports about Homosexuality – Anglican, Roman Catholic and Methodist – from the Friends Homosexual Fellowship. (As always with the Quakers, one has to make clear that this is not an official 'Party Line' – which doesn't exist – but the consensus of a particular group following a peculiar mode of discussion.) The Friends group rates the reports in the order Methodists, Anglicans and Roman Catholics. But it complains of all of them that the actual *experience* of homosexuals, whether Christian or otherwise, is seldom taken into account. The element of personal experience is central to Quakers, and the group insists that homosexual people can testify to the blessing and strength they receive from their relationships, however much they may be told they are sinful and ought to be overcome. 'For many people', says the group, 'difficulties arise because homosexual relationships confuse the boundaries of friendship and marriage . . .' And surely that is a very penetrating remark, wherever it may lead.

The Church of Scotland has been thinking about the relationship between belonging to the church and belonging to a trade union, and has published a trim little booklet on the subject. Christians, it thinks, ought to belong to their union, and are often better employed attending union meetings than kirk sessions. It does not think that disputes or strikes are necessarily evil: conflict challenges both sides to think again and find a better basis for working together. And the working party that produced this report is fairly hard-headed about conscience and the closed shop. The issue, it says, is very seldom a straightforward contest between the man of principle and the trade union steamroller: the Bible does not equate personal freedom with self-centred individualism. No wonder the booklet gets an approving foreword from Mr Len Murray.

For the time being, then, that's all you'll be hearing from me – unless a runner breaks through the undergrowth of Portland Place bearing a tape recording in a cleft stick. A whole lot more letters will have to go unanswered, I'm afraid: and even one telegram that arrived recently from Saffron Walden. It said: 'Please keep God alive otherwise millions of parsons and you will be on the dole.' Dear Listener, it's not a question of *me* keeping *him* alive – and if clergy pay is as bad as they say, the dole might be a leg up.

The Pipul Tree

10 January 1981

Good morning again. It's good to be back in familiar company, to find on my desk that anonymous box of chocolates some kind listener has been sending me every year, the Christmas cards and the letters. I really must pay attention to the one that says: 'I'm sure you're a very nice man, but you come over like a pompous twit which I find very irritating . . .' Ah, bring back Rosemary Hartill, I hear you cry – and who am I to disagree?

For almost six weeks, I've been chugging slowly round India by train – a sentimental pilgrimage in memory of the days when I worked there as the BBC's correspondent. For part of the trip, I stayed in a small university town called Serampore, on the banks of the Ganges upriver from Calcutta. The college was founded more than 160 years ago by Carey, Marshman and Ward, the Northamptonshire Baptist missionaries, and today it trains ministers from all over India. Still a tiny island upon an ocean of Hinduism, Serampore has much to be proud of – as has the missionary endeavour in general; but it is no use pretending that the Christian Church is ever likely to become more than one among India's minority faiths. To me, the experience of sitting on that island, surveying the ocean around it, was a profound lesson in looking outwards from Christianity into Hinduism and trying to understand God's will in this. A lesson, among other things, in humility.

The house I was staying in had a balcony, and every morning I was drawn out to it to watch how the average Bengali practised his worship. On the river bank, across the road, stood a Pipul Tree with its knotted trunk and graceful quivering leaves. The Pipul Tree has been sacred for thousands of years, for the god Vishnu was born under one, and the Buddha achieved Enlightenment as he sat beneath one. This particular Pipul was especially sacred; for out of one side of it sprouted a Banyan Tree, with trailing aerial roots, and at its feet someone had built a little shrine, just a few inches high, with a stone knob representing the god Shiva and a small carving of the bull Nandi crouching before it. In the tree there lived a large grey monkey who descended to tease the herds of goats which came to drink from the river, and then – when the goat boys chased him – would throw himself into the arms of the old man who sat all day on a stone bench nearby, the monkey's protector. There also lived in the tree two shabby vultures, which came flapping down to feast on the carrion the river washed up. Holy the Ganges may be – anyone who dies within sight of it goes straight to Heaven, and the banks are littered with pavilions to come and die in and burning grounds for cremation – but its swiftly moving khaki-coloured waters convey an unappetizing stew of corpses, dead dogs, open sewerage and effluent from the nearby jute mills. Nevertheless, being sacred, it would be blasphemous to suggest that the Ganges could be impure.

And so every morning, as dawn broke, I watched the people come down to its banks for their morning bath. Modestly wrapped in cotton cloth they bobbed and bowed in the river, sipped and splashed it with hands folded in prayer, and then emerged with a brass pot of holy water to water the roots of the Pipul Tree, wash the little shrine, and, facing downriver, bow to the rising sun.

Paganism? Idolatry? If you like. But I found it moving, soothing and full of faith: the river of time watched over by the tree of life, and the simple folk of Serampore acknowledging the God in both. Remembering Jordan, surely no Christian should find the use of water strange. And recalling Eden, recalling how our very churches are built to imitate the sacred groves, what's wrong with using a living tree – rather than a dead one – as the symbol of life eternal? Argue if you will that the faith brought to Serampore by Carey and his friends was a higher one than Hinduism. But what I can't accept now is that God was not already there, had not always been there, on the banks of the Ganges, though in a different guise from that in which he revealed himself to us.

Beggar, My Neighbour

17 January 1981

As I was saying last time, I've recently got back from six weeks travelling round India – a country I worked in as a correspondent more than twenty years ago. Very little has changed since then; least of all, perhaps, the condition of the poor – though one missionary I stayed with told me he thought there was rather more destitution now than there had been in the 1950s. But I don't know how you could measure that.

So many visitors to India are rapidly sickened by the squalor, poverty and human degradation around them – above all, by the swarms of lepers, cripples and beggars who pester them for *Baksheesh*. Such visitors find it hard to understand how I could actually enjoy India, find it so richly rewarding in spite of everything. Can it be that I've developed a kind of imperialist immunity to pity?

For I have to admit that – while I was never unaware of the poverty, or of the more abstract problems of the Third World – it did not *shock* me, paralyse me, or kill off my conviction of the goodness and fatherhood of God. Partly, I suppose, I was used to it. The mind has to develop a way of coping with it or you simply cannot go on, let alone do a job of reporting. To be brutally practical, bursting into tears does not help anybody. Trying to figure out the meaning of it all may.

India is full of horror stories and it's not surprising that Indians resent having them told. The deepening corruption of business and politics, the brutality of the police, the bigotry of caste Hindus and dark atrocities like widow-burning and dowry extortion might be held to invalidate any claim India might have to preach to the rest of us. But we all have our horror stories, display to others our often unconscious hypocrisy. It seems to me the reporter must refuse to say, 'Look at these subhuman animals!', and look instead for our brothers and sisters under the skin.

I'm going to be misunderstood anyway, so here goes: it is certainly no fun to be poor in India – and yet the poor do have their fun. Dreadful though it may seem to you and me, they know where they belong and they make the most of it. A troupe of beggars putting on their act for the tourist may be heartbreaking; many of them are real professionals at it and hire a cripple in a barrow as an added attraction. Watch them off duty, gossiping, planning their strategy, bedding down for the night, and they emerge not as projections of *your* guilt and embarrassment, but as lively human beings in their own right, with their own dignity and humour. More than once, I've seen homeward-going schoolchildren fling down their books to do a spot of freelance begging and roar with laughter when I've caught them out.

One of the agonies suffered by the foreign visitor is, 'How can I possibly give to them all?' Simply keeping enough small change is a constant problem. But outside the great temples there are often *Baksheesh* changers: you hand over one rupee (worth six pence) and get back twenty or thirty small coins. A couple of these satisfy a beggar's honour and win you merit, which is what the rules of the game require. For you are not expected to keep the entire beggar population in affluence, or even one of them (which would be unfair on the others).

I don't imagine this will acquit me of the charge of callousness, but I do plead not guilty. It often seems to me that tender-hearted folk spend much time debating what we should do for – or often to – the Third World in order to make it more like ours, but very little considering the here and now of today's poor (which is what Mother Teresa is all about). Watching the poor of India making cowdung patties for fuel, picking individual blades of grass for fodder, washing their rags in stagnant puddles, you realize that they are people engaged like you in the business of living – not as *you* would live or as they *should* live – but miraculously coping in a way which I doubt whether we could devise. We would expect revolt and the massacre of millions, but India's humble and meek count their blessings on the fingers of one leprous hand.

Thomas of India

24 January 1981

This is the last of my notes on a recent visit to India; and lest you think I've gone completely pagan, it deals with the legend – or is it fact? – that Christianity was brought to India by the Apostle Thomas and that he was martyred and buried near Madras.

The intriguing thing about St Thomas as a gospel figure is that he is little more than a name in Matthew, Mark and Luke, but he plays a key role in John. It is he who volunteers to be killed with Jesus, he who calls forth the declaration 'I am the way and the truth', and it is he – Doubting Thomas – who is shown the wounds of the Risen Christ. In apocryphal literature he has a gospel of his own and a fantastic history known as the Acts of Thomas – both of them go back to the third century, and both are tainted with obscure heresies.

But despite the fantasy, the Acts of Thomas do contain certain plausible elements. They tell how the disciples drew lots for the world and India fell to the unwilling Thomas; how Thomas was recruited as a carpenter by King Gondophares; how he preached and converted through all India, and eventually fell into the hands of a King Mazdai who had him put to death with spears upon a mountain top. The bones of the martyr were later carried off to the West, first to Edessa and then Ortona.

Now there really was a King Gondophares in Northwest India at about the right time, not too far from Parthia (or Persia), which is where another tradition places our apostle. But there are no traces of early Christians left there. The churches which today claim St Thomas as their founder are all in the extreme South of India where trade routes across the Arabian Sea did bring merchants from the Middle East, including the so-called Black Jews of Cranganore. Thomas is said to have landed there in A.D. 52; and when the Roman Catholic Portuguese arrived on the Malabar coast almost fifteen hundred years later, they were shocked to find a fully developed, non-Catholic church using ancient Syrian as its language.

It's true there had been arrivals of Syrians in the fifth century. But even before that, the Western churches agreed St Thomas had died in India. King Alfred the Great sent offerings to his shrine, and later explorers like Marco Polo confirmed its existence. It was the Portuguese who actually opened the tomb in 1523, to find – deep underground – some bones, a spearhead and a pottery bowl filled with blood-stained earth. The site was at Mylapore, today a seaside suburb of Madras.

It may, of course, be a pious – if ancient – fraud. There is nothing very inspiring about the place today: a large tropical-gothic basilica dated 1896, and beneath the altar a kind of well with a grille over it, through which you can see the red, sandy earth. The bones and spear are kept locked up.

There are two other places, not far off, which help to fill out the story. The first is the Little Mount, on which stands a small Portuguese village church with a cave under it. Early Christians had a passion for caves. It was here, they say, that Thomas was praying when his enemies found him and wounded him in the thigh. He fled about two miles to what is known as the Great – or St Thomas's – Mount, where he was executed.

Today you slog up 130 steps to the Mount – quite a penance in the thick Madras heat – handing out small coins to ecumenical beggars along its Via Dolorosa. At the top there's a Franciscan home for underprivileged babies, and another old Portuguese church which exhibits what is claimed to be St Thomas's altar cross, but which is probably ninth-century Nestorian. For some reason Thomas attracts heresies. I doubt if the Malabar churches are really as old as they say, but that does not prove St Thomas was never there. After all, why invent so remote a mission for him? Today his churches claim as high an ancestry as any in Europe, and as much evidence that Thomas died in Madras as that Peter died in Rome.

Lesser Breeds Without

31 January 1981

You will find almost no difference at all between two documents issued early this week by the Roman Catholic Archbishops of England and Wales and the Board for Social Responsibility of the Church of England: whatever their doctrinal distinctions, the two churches are entirely at one over the Government's British Nationality Bill, setting up a three-tier system of citizenship. In this they have the endorsement of the British Council of Churches, the Board of Deputies of British Jews and the Joint Council for the Welfare of Immigrants – all of which have expressed grave concern both over the unfairness of the Bill, as they see it, and over the resentment and suspicion they believe it will cause.

Now resentment and suspicion are not, of course, all on one side. If there's a criticism to be made of the churches in this matter, it is that they take the attitude 'Racism is wrong' and say very little to acknowledge or calm the anxieties that many of their rank and file members surely do feel about the strangers in their midst. The Roman Catholics and Anglicans both want the Bill to state that Britain's national identity is now multi-racial. That's probably a fact and it may even be right, but a lot of people will be murmuring 'Oh no it isn't!' So far as the leadership of the churches is concerned, that viewpoint is brushed aside, maybe for the best of moral reasons, but with some risk of becoming detached from those who are being led.

However, if one is to report what the churches (as institutions) are saying, they are saying only one thing: that the Nationality Bill is wrong and ought at least to be drastically amended; and to be fair, they have not said that without opportunities for discussion and debate.

In their letter to the Home Secretary, Cardinal Hume and his fellow archbishops have protested at the abandonment of the ancient *Jus Soli* – that anyone born on British soil thereby acquires British nationality. There is no guarantee that Commonwealth citizens already living here will have their civic rights preserved. Members of minority groups who were born here will face more frequent questioning of their status. And those who are classified British Overseas Citizens or Citizens of Dependent Territories will have no right of entry or residence anywhere, say the Archbishops; indeed, they are liable to find themselves virtually stateless. The Roman Catholics' letter reminds Mr Whitelaw that the Bill gives him powers which he can exercise without appeal or explanation. The Church of England, in its public statement, concludes: 'The Bill is not intended to provide an intelligible and defensible basis for citizenship rights . . . In effect it provides a rationale in nationality law for the immigration legislation of the past two decades, which is frankly discriminatory, on racial grounds.'

Assuming the Government believes it has a popular mandate for the Bill, the churches' attitude will be *un*popular. If they need biblical justification, they could point to the Book of Leviticus: 'The stranger that dwelleth with you shall be unto you as one born among you and thou shalt love him as thyself.' Yes, that is a Jewish saying, the Jewish community is grateful Britain has applied it to Jews, and disturbed we seem to be wavering. Some might say we are questioning not only a duty but a gift and a privilege. Be that as it may, another quite different conclusion stands out as well, that the churches have now learnt to co-ordinate their views and to speak out fearlessly to the political establishment on the basis of not what they think is expedient but what they believe is right. That is an element we need in our deliberations, and from where else can we hear it?

Marry or Burn?

7 February 1981

It shouldn't happen to a Cardinal, especially not to Cardinal Basil Hume, the Benedictine monk. 'WHY I'D WED' yapped the *Daily Mirror*. 'I YEARN FOR A WIFE' titivated the *Sun*. 'MARRIAGE AND MY SACRIFICE' tear-jerked the *Daily Express*, also mentioning the end of the Archbishop's squash-playing career.

Maybe the articles weren't quite up to the headlines, but it emerged that sometimes the Cardinal had felt it would have been nice to have a wife to confide in, but that was one of the sacrifices one had to make and he was a firm believer that priests ought to be celibate so that they could devote their lives to God. The quotations actually came from a documentary for Thames Television. Cardinal Hume was evidently impressed by the film, but so startled by the papers (which I thought made him sound rather human) that he put out a statement deploring their trivialization and making it clear that, in his view, celibacy had deep roots in the Western Catholic tradition. I have no doubt the Cardinal believes in it sincerely and is anxious that his priests and people should know that. But I don't think he need have worried. Pope John Paul II may be a vigorous defender of the celibate priesthood; but I doubt if he reads the *Sun* or even the *Guardian*.

I'm told there's a vogue for celibacy in the United States these days – though I'm not sure I believe it, for nowhere has the Church suffered heavier losses than it has in America from priests quitting to marry. In Western Europe, too, the groan goes up: 'Why can't we marry? Apart from the personal agony, how else can we share the lives of our people and be fully human like them?' To which Cardinal Hume himself has replied, 'My sole guiding light is Christ our Lord, whom I accept as being both fully human and celibate.' But remember, the Cardinal was speaking then as an abbot to his monks.

The Bible is ambivalent on the matter. The Jews were and are appalled by celibacy. Some of the apostles were married; and while St Paul rather favours celibacy and virginity, he does say that he has no instructions from the

Lord, and he allows married bishops. Jesus himself (in Matthew 19) presents celibacy as a consecration to God, but not compulsory. It seems to have remained a voluntary choice during the early generations of the Church.

Somewhere around the fourth century an East-West split developed. In the East it was accepted that monastics, who often went on to be bishops, must not marry, while the parish clergy could and even should be married. And so it remains among the Orthodox to the present day. In the West, it was decreed as early as the year 306 that all married clergy must leave their wives and not father children – a harsh ruling tempered by Leo the Great a century later, but only with the concession that the couple must live together as brother and sister. Later still, married men were only ordained after exchanging with their wives a mutual vow of chastity, after which the wife often entered a nunnery.

For many centuries, however, there was hanky-panky in the presbytery. From time to time, efforts were made to stamp out clerical concubinage: notably the Gregorian Reform of the early twelfth century, which again had much to do with the monastic revival then going on. Apart from anything else, the Church was getting fed up with married priests leaving *its* property to *their* sons. Things were pretty lax again by the fifteenth century and had to be tightened up by the Council of Trent, which had the Protestant example to stand against. There have been very few exceptions made, for example those of the Uniate Churches, and of certain married Anglicans who had 'gone over to Rome'. Yet the pressure for married priests is building up once more.

Myself, I can see both sides. I see with awe the sacrifice that's made and the dedication it produces. I see with some horror the way certain Catholic priests still expect to be waited on by women. I see the eagerness to be an icon of

Christ, and the objectivity that celibacy can bring. Sex ain't everything. But neither is unvarying tradition. I can't help feeling the Orthodox have got it about right, and no one could accuse them of trendiness. Must every priest be also a monk?

Animal Crackers

14 February 1981

Next to my wife's, of course, there's no opinion I value more highly than that of the *Church Times* columnist Margaret Duggan. So that when Mrs Duggan gave Volume Two of the collected *Yours Faithfully* an even better review than Volume One, adding a constructive suggestion at the end, I hasten to respond. What she said was that I had not yet come to grips with the relationship of Man with the Animals, perhaps because I had been diverted from the real issues by some of the hysterical mail one tends to get from the animal lobby. Which is probably true; though there are other reasons, too, for my reluctance to go overboard for animals, or indeed for anything else. As a matter of self-preservation, as well as that famous if unfashionable virtue objectivity, I think it is rather important to stay inside the boat we all share.

I have a theory that somewhere on the skin of everybody there's an invisible button which – when touched even ever-so-lightly – switches on his or her personal mania; though each of us is convinced that in our own case it is entirely reasonable and right. Margaret Duggan may have identified mine correctly as a romantic view of womanhood which is rather unliberated. In others (I have observed) it can be anything from Pacifism to Fluoride, Astrology to

Vivisection, Vegetarianism to the Literal Truth of the Bible. Each of us has a cause tucked away in our knapsack, a banner behind the front door. Things as a whole are too much for us to cope with, but maybe we could – by concentrating our energies and teaming up with other single-minded spirits – make *some* impression on (say) Disarmament or the Deforestation of the countryside. (Now there's a neglected cause to go batty about! Trees!)

All of these are admirable causes in themselves. But I turn now to President Carter's farewell broadcast. There was, he said, a danger from 'single interest groups' which sought to ensure that whatever else happened, their own personal views and interests were protected. 'This', said Mr Carter, 'is a disturbing factor in American political life. It tends to distort our purposes because the national interest is not always the same as the sum of our single or special interests.' I think we are less susceptible to that kind of manipulation in Britain because we are less of a democracy, but we are not altogether immune. The lure of the simple answer, the direct solution, grows stronger the more discordant life becomes. And to nobody is it more tempting than to the religious-minded. The Gospel appears to offer simple solutions in every other verse.

It appears to, but it doesn't. The disciples were constantly bewildered by Christ's teachings, and by the whole Gospel and its message to the whole man. For my money, the real heroes of the faith are not those who barricade themselves behind a closed system, but those who are open to the uncertainties, dilemmas and temptations of our paganized, urbanized life, and who *compromise*. The notion of a Christian compromising may sound shocking. There must be points where he won't – though he risks cutting himself off there. But a God who became Man, enjoyed the company of publicans and sinners and was a notorious rule-breaker can hardly have been narrow-minded. He had his principles (to death, in fact) but he was not one to avoid the richness of life or, so far as I can tell, to get hung up on personal taboos.

But whatever became of the relationship between Man and the Animals? It doesn't look as if Mrs Duggan is going to get her deep theology this time, either. But what I am trying to say is that a balance, a compromise, a co-existence based on caring and respect must lie at the heart of it; not a doting sentimentality nor a ruthless exploitation, even if the resulting middle road disappoints the single-issue lobby. The animals are in trust to us from our Creator, and I think we need them as a matter of mental health as well as of ecological survival. But then we, too, are in trust to ourselves and to each other. We do not serve God by narrowing our minds, by cutting each other out.

Pick of the Week

21 February 1981

The pick of next week's religious broadcasting has to be – surprise! surprise! – the General Synod of the Church of England. The key man in every broadcasting network is the scheduling planner, the expert who cunningly places the star attraction at the right point every day; and whoever scheduled this session of Synod may have a future in broadcasting – for there isn't a day without its headlined feature.

It all begins, on Monday, with a vote on how to vote. Unlike the House of Commons across the road, on important issues Synod can desert the simple majority system and require (say) a two-thirds majority in each of its three divisions – bishops, clergy and laity. And that is what's being proposed for final approval of the famous Covenant for Unity with the Methodists, United Reformed and other Free Churches. Fair enough, you may say, for a treaty of such solemnity: but behind it lies the calculation that the more conservative clergy may be able to frustrate (for deeply spiritual reasons, no doubt) what the laity and bishops are more likely to approve.

The Covenant itself comes up on Wednesday, and members have been bombarded with letters and petitions either imploring them to take the great leap forward, or warning them to stay where they are. The permanent department concerned (the Board for Mission and Unity) has commended the Covenant and urged Synod not to delay or substantially amend. It's pointed out that the Covenant will not instantly build a single uniform church, and that the churches – though reconciled – will remain separate entities. The attitude of Anglican Catholics will be crucial. Many of them fear that moving closer to the Free Churches will mean moving further from the Romans and Orthodox: though it has to be said, first that union with Rome is far from being just round the corner, and second that the Roman Church in England has positively encouraged the others to forge the Covenant. At best, however, the Covenant will be referred by Synod to the dioceses for another fifteen months.

Tuesday's star attraction has just been through that process: it's the so-called Lichfield Report on Marriage and the Church's task, or (in journalese) what to do about divorced Christians who remarry or want to remarry in church. Back in 1978, Synod fell back on its favourite escape route saying it would be 'inappropriate' to make any change in the rules, and the dioceses were evenly divided, so that's likely to stand. Which means, I suspect, that an increasing number of clergy will use their own discretion under Common Law to remarry the divorced, or that Anglicans will avail themselves of the services offered by Free Churches and the State. Synod will be asked to relax the rules against ordaining divorced men or allowing divorced clergy to continue in parish work, and its rules on Communion for the divorced.

Thursday's 'great debate' is on unemployment: something you might not have thought the Church could do much about. In conscience, though, it refuses to turn its back on the problem, and its Industrial Committee has rounded up some intriguing facts and figures. Without in the least belittling the problem, it finds that more than half of the unemployed move within three months into expanding industries. At the more depressing end it notes the growing number of long-term unemployed.

And on Friday, the inevitable Sex Debate: Homosexual Relationships (and let us hope the classically-minded Synod remembers it's the Greek *Homoios* not the Latin *Homo*). The Gloucester Report on the subject pleased nobody; the fact is, there's no consensus in the Church; and though some members want to disown Gloucester, the official line is to 'take note of it' and file it away in some dark crypt.

Which leaves us with minor bits and pieces. The Reverend Michael Saward (one of your collar-and-tie vicars) wants freedom of clerical dress, except on canonical occasions. The Reverend P.W. Wheatley votes a cheer for next year's visit from the Pope. And the Reverend M.R. Hodge of Rochester thinks it is high time we took the role of Godparents more seriously. I wonder if there are any ears tingling guiltily at that?

A Third Programme

28 February 1981

A weighty BBC document fell on my desk the other day, and it contained the following comment about the followers and critics of Radio 3 (which I still think of as 'The Third Programme'). 'Some of them', it observed, 'treat the network as a cultural Church of England, to be preserved, cherished and defended, yet used less assiduously.' A stimulating remark when you turn it the other way round. Just think of the Church of England as a kind of ecclesiastical Radio 3, with music, scholarly talks, an establishment rating out of all proportion to the numbers attending, and a high-powered outcry at the slightest hint of redundancy. You can pick your own equivalents to the other channels.

But whatever the BBC decides to do, the churches are thinking of merging their networks. Last Wednesday, the General Synod of the Church of England voted to consult its diocesan synods about the proposed Covenant for Unity with the Free Churches. The voting was complex, but in a very full house indeed you could say that the essential principle of the Covenant was approved by 364 votes to 155. The snag is that, had this been the final vote, it would have failed by six votes to have got the necessary two-thirds of the clergy. The failure would have been slightly worse on the issue of women Free Church ministers. Whether the margin will narrow or widen in the next eighteen months, we can only wait and see. I would say the prospects for the Covenant are somewhat better than I had previously thought; but there is going to be a good deal of agony in the months ahead.

For despite several assertions that the Free Churches had been generous in their concessions and that the Church of England could not expect anything closer to its terms, the word soon spread that further amendments might yet be possible. This cat was unbagged among the pigeons by the Archbishop of Canterbury himself. Rejecting the 'now or never – one last heave' theory, he told Synod that he did not expect to see the proposals back again in their present form. In a very subtle speech, Dr Runcie said he had mixed feelings about covenanting. He did not agree that it would cut off the Church of England from the Roman Catholics and the Orthodox, but he dreaded the 'energy-consuming bureaucratic quagmire' that lay in store under the promise of joint decision-making among the churches. 'Frankly', he added, 'the Covenant will require from us a deeper faith in Divine Grace.'

'Truth is not negotiable', said the Archdeacon of Leicester. 'Minorities are dictating to us', said Father Geldard. And the Dean of St Albans damned the Covenant as 'a vague Common Market of churches'. The most sombre of speeches came from the Bishop of Southwell, who said 'The number of churches we are *not* covenanting with – the ones with the strongest convictions – grows every day. The Church of England is in danger of believing in nothing.' The Bishop declared the whole enterprise was wrong and counter-productive. Schemes only created greater *dis*unity. All he wanted was intercommunion.

On the opposite side, the Archbishop of York sturdily demolished the myth of an unbroken succession of bishops from the time of the apostles; and the Archdeacon of Rochester held up local examples of ecumenism actually working. They began very legalistically, but 'as our fears and suspicions begin to die away, there comes a point where you realize you have become one', he said.

Curiously, nobody said in so many words, 'How can we not ask the people?' The people, I suppose, aren't in the apostolic succession. I must say, if restrained passion had been decisive, the Noes would have had it. Dr Leonard, the Bishop of Truro, seemed almost ill with the pain of it, as he accused himself of having allowed the covenanters to make a false separation between Faith and Order. But the contradictions had not been settled – they had within them the seeds of Division. For a moment, some of us in the gallery wondered if Dr Leonard was on the verge of resigning his See, as he declared tragically: 'In the interests of Unity, we are prepared to see one-third of our number go to the wall!'

Bless This House

14 March 1981

There are times when, try as you may, you can't help your private life overwhelming your public responsibilities. Maybe I ought to be talking this week about Anglican-Roman Unity, or the Budget or the Black Community; but the truth is I can't focus on anything but the fact that I have just been moving house, and it has been one of the great crises of middle life, rather (I imagine) like getting divorced and remarried simultaneously. I tried to explain it in those very terms to Cardinal Hume, when I ran into him at the very height of the upheaval, and I realize now it wasn't the most appropriate of similes to offer to a Roman Catholic monk who has renounced marriage, divorce, home and possessions. But it goes to show how the experience unnerves one. I must say, as always, the Cardinal was most sympathetic about it.

Since I have embarked on this fragment of autobiography, I had better fill in some more details. After years of living abroad, my wife and I came back to London with four children and solved our housing problem by purchasing my mother-in-law's house from her. As our children grew up and left home, it took only a couple of sums on the backs of envelopes to demonstrate, to *my* satisfaction anyway, that we ought to move to a smaller house. But we liked the neighbourhood – we have loyal friends round there, not to mention our doctor and our Quaker Meeting and all the shops and walks we've grown accustomed to; so it was a matter of waiting until a smaller house came onto the market as close as possible to the old one. Eventually it did – only three doors round the corner – and there were loud jeers from the children of 'Why don't you go to a *fun* place? Covent Garden! The Barbican! Limehouse!' 'We don't *know* anyone there', we said. 'Besides the cats wouldn't like it.'

And so we moved, three doors round the corner, and it almost broke my wife's heart as twenty years of beloved family junk had to be ruthlessly weeded out and heaved into the council lorry; and as strangers (most agreeable ones, I'm glad to say, as circumstances have made them neighbours as well as purchasers) prowled our hallowed halls, plotting, no doubt, drastic alterations. Don't tell me the only difference between men and women is the roles imposed on them by society; and don't tell me either that men are the ones with the territorial imperative. I like to think that *I* was perfectly objective about the move; that it stands to reason two people need a smaller heap of bricks than six do. What I failed to realize was what those bricks meant to my wife in terms of births, deaths and marriages, of children safely reared and still cared for, of storms weathered, of shelter always there. And not to let this sound excessively maternal, of hospitality shared, books written and prints made on the 1897 Albion press in the dining-room.

The press has been reassembled round the corner, my typewriter's waiting and there are spare beds for the children. But it will take another few years before the new home is home like the old home. The cats still won't accept it and perch gloomily outside the one we've left.

Where's the religious angle? Well, I am far too fortunate for it to sound anything but hypocritical if I embarked on a lament for the homeless. But the experience has taught me a lesson about how deep the community of love can go, and about how love can sanctify a place, soak into its very walls. And I wonder how it was for Christ's mother when he left home; and for Christ himself when he abandoned his house in Capernaum and took up the life of a wandering preacher. To be without home or family must require desperate strength; for it is to leave oneself totally open and vulnerable. At home we are masters of our own fate, with a right to be loved and cared for, and clear duties as to whom we should care for and love. A mere house is not a home. It takes a mysterious – perhaps sacramental – conspiracy of the material and the spiritual to make a home, and more often than not it seems to be women who make it, and men who break it.

Soul of the Party

21 March 1981

We seem to be living in a period of polarization. Activists of all kinds are becoming more and more insistent upon their own rightness (or leftness), less and less tolerant of those in the middle of the road. That curious word 'wet' (with its overtones of a prep-school dormitory) is slapped in people's faces on the one hand, while on the other the clinching non-argument is that such-and-such is 'middle class'. Across the Atlantic it has been asserted that *détente* is dead, and that if you don't support the regimes the US government supports, you are probably a communist. To those of us who followed the disaster of Vietnam down its long, bloody slope, the precedents are depressing.

What? Politics in religion again – or non-rightwing and therefore presumably leftwing politics? But that is one of the fallacies. For a start, Christians are in politics because political things happen to them whether they like it or not, and they are bound to ask themselves how their faith should affect their reactions. But beyond that, we have only to watch Jesus at work in the gospels to realize that even in his political situation – which was radically polarized – he assessed people as individuals in their own right, not as labelled categories, not as party members. So there may be righteous leftwingers, rightwingers and members of the centre. It has been suggested that the new Social Democrat Party in Britain is the natural party for Christians trying to avoid being driven to extremes. One can see the argument, but I think it would be a pity if it became so, because surely Christians ought to be rather unreliable members of any party. Sometimes they should be saying, 'We cannot talk as if the other parties were demons', and at others they should insist, 'That may be a party decision, but a higher authority says No.' Conscience, of course, is both a wet and rather bourgeois concept – but not to the Church.

Jesus shocked his contemporaries by teaching – and showing – that we should love not just the neighbours in our own community, but also our enemies the Roman army of occupation: the military regime as well as the freedom fighters, the freedom fighters as well as the military regime. It was an objectivity which should prompt Christians to view and criticize both on equal terms, regardless of their labels. The violence and oppression of the one side cannot escape judgement any more than that of the other. No amount of communist threat can justify torture and liquidation; no amount of police repression can justify terrorism (though there are honest Christians who would say that open warfare is another matter). Movements that employ such methods – sturdy and unbourgeois though they may be – make a Christ of every victim they abuse and crucify, and that is as true in the labour camps of Siberia as it is in the interrogation cells of Latin America.

Amnesty International and Friends House have recently published a small but cogent pamphlet by Eric Baker entitled *Public Policy and the Use of Torture*, which points out that torture – or 'interrogation in depth' – is always sought to be justified by reference to the motives of the interrogator rather than to the sufferings of the victim: a cruel necessity to procure vital information, save innocent lives and defend the State. Eric Baker writes: 'It is a sober truth that such moral progress as the human race has made has been in proportion to the extent that it has allowed its desire for quick, cheap results to be restrained by its respect for the helpless.' And he cites the principle of the German philosopher Kant, that men should never be treated as means but only as ends in themselves.

And here, I think, is the deepest danger of polarization: that it tempts us to the conclusion that the end – the party's end, the nation's end – does justify the means. I'm not offering one over-simplification in place of another: Christians are in a very uncomfortable situation, for the side they have to take cuts across the convenient geometry of right and left. And most of those involved in a tragedy like Vietnam or El Salvador have very little choice as to side. I may not, in all this, be striking a particularly virile attitude; but perhaps we still need liberating from political virility.

The Laughter of God

28 March 1981

Must religion always be solemn? Is there such a thing as the Laughter of God? Let me tell you a story:

The first man in space was Colonel Yuri Gagarin of the Red Army. When he returned to Earth there was a big reception at the Kremlin, and Khrushchev (then leader of the Communist Party) drew the Colonel to one side. 'Tell me, Comrade Gagarin,' he demanded, 'when you were up in the heavens, did you see God?' Colonel Gagarin looked nervously over his shoulder and then whispered, 'Nikita Sergeivitch, I must tell you – I did.' 'Alas!' exclaimed Khrushchev. 'It is just as I feared! But tell nobody!' Then the heroic Cosmonaut was dispatched on a world tour; and eventually he came to Rome and was invited to the Vatican. The Pope drew him to one side. 'Tell me, Colonel Gagarin – when you were in the heavens, did you see God?' And Colonel Gagarin, remembering his orders replied: 'Holy Father, I must tell you – I did not.' 'Alas!' cried the Pope. 'It is just as I feared! But tell nobody!'

Like all my best religious stories, I heard that one from a Rabbi. There is something about the Jewish faith – and I suppose it is their need to survive the unsurvivable, to bear the intolerable – that generates a steady undercurrent of laughter, for fear of weeping. And it is this collision of opposites that lies at the heart of laughter. What is funny about the Colonel Gagarin story is the incongruity, the incoherence, of the Communist leader who believes in God and the Pope who doesn't. They don't fit, they don't belong together, and the only way our mind can cope with the situation is to wipe it all out in an explosion of laughter. But I would suggest something further: that, in a way, our laughter is a shout of relief – relief at discovering the universe is not all cut and dried and logical, as we really know it is not. For if it were, then the Popes and Khrushchevs of this world would have it all wrapped up and organized, and there would be no freedom of thought and venture for the rest of us. 'Thank God', we are saying, 'for absurdity and mystery.'

Thank God. But the joke I told, while it was a joke involving God, was hardly God's joke. Could we ascribe to him anything so human as a confession of the absurdity of things? Well, if we believe in the Incarnation it is certainly not impossible for God to enter into our feelings as well as our flesh. If he can suffer, he can laugh as well. It is hard to find many jokes in the Bible – laughter and fools tend to be lumped together – but I can't believe that Jesus, who enjoyed the company of publicans and sinners and was a notorious party-goer, never laughed. A laughterless Christ would not have been the full, true man we believe him to be. Don't tell me he had no sense of joy.

But God's laughter would surely rule out some of the forms of laughter we indulge in – cruel laughter, thoughtless or dirty laughter. Laughter that degrades, perverts, humiliates would not be on his lips. But there is loving and affectionate laughter. There can be affection in our laughter even when we are laughing *at* our neighbour for something ridiculous – when we recognize ourselves in our neighbour, when we share that common experience.

In that good laughter – the laughter of joy and relief at

recognizing we are one after all, and that the grimly mechanical view of life has broken down – there is something profoundly 'of God'. He is somewhere at the bottom of it. There is a harmony and unity we cannot otherwise explain. In spite of the confusion, things are going as Nature intended them; and when they do, I am quite sure that God laughs too. In a way, this is the very opposite of the laughter of disjointedness I first spoke of. The two opposites meet together at the back, perhaps because they do both reveal to us the same thing – our fundamental unity under the mystery of God, which is the greatest of reliefs and releases.

But does God have any private jokes of his own? I suspect that many of our efforts to worship him on Sunday must send him into happy convulsions; and our efforts to define who he is in language that simply cannot contain him. 'Missed again!' he cries. 'Not that! Not that!' What can be more laughable than people who cannot know pretending that they do?

A Tale of Three Cities

4 April 1981

I must begin with an apology for letters unanswered. The fact is, I'm travelling a lot these days collecting interviews, so there hasn't been much time for the 'In' tray.

The most obviously ecclesiastical event of a heavily headlined week was the nomination of Dr Graham Leonard of Truro to be Bishop of London – though it gathered some of the atmosphere of the election of a fourteenth-century Pope. As a vigorous Anglican Catholic with a fine record of pastoral care, Dr Leonard has been in line for promotion for some years past. Traditionally High Church London might seem the obvious place for him. He was a City rector, Archdeacon of Hampstead, then suffragan Bishop of Willesden, and as chairman of the Board for Social Responsibility he knows the corridors of Church House and has grappled with most of the issues of the day. Who better to be the Church of England's spokesman in the House of Lords?

On the other hand, Dr Leonard is a conservative (his critics would say reactionary) on issues like women priests, homosexuality, remarriage of the divorced and Church Unity, in a city where progressive views are loudly expressed. A 'Stop Leonard' movement dug itself in. It would appear that the Appointments Commission – set up to advise the Prime Minister on the choice of bishops – wanted John Habgood of Durham; but was outflanked by Dr Leonard's admirers outside. We are assured there was nothing improper in this and that the Leonard Lobby was, indeed, more in tune with the desires of the London parishes than was the Commission. Let us hope so; and that London's new bishop will be enthroned with charity on the one hand and generosity on the other. But it is a pity that the new system, which had worked so smoothly in earlier cases, has now been opened to charges of manipulation and politicking. However, such is the penalty of secrecy. And can you really expect to remain the Established Church and escape the attentions of the Establishment?

But this will seem small beer to most people compared with the shooting of President Reagan. It so happens that I would admit to being pro American, but it's hard to stand up to the torrent of sarcastic comments like 'That country of violence where they shoot presidents like other people shoot rats – and won't even take the guns away from lunatics!' Well, that's fair enough as far as it goes – which isn't very far. It doesn't explain how guns became so widespread, or how anyone could get rid of them now, or the outrage that many Americans would feel if government attempted to do so: which has to do with an intense, if primitive, sense of the right of a free citizen to protect himself against all comers and not trust authority to do it for him.

No, of course that is not my personal view: thank God for our relative freedom from the curse of the gun. But it's not so easy to hold to the other extreme and say that violence is always wrong. What about the official violence of the commandos (the Indonesian equivalents of the SAS) who stormed the airliner at Bangkok and defeated the latest hijacking? The British government sent congratulations, probably feeling the operation atoned for the terrorist triumph in the previous hijacking of a Pakistani plane. Should the Indonesians have given in for the sake of short-term non-violence? Or would that just have encouraged the others? Is it better to risk losing a few innocent passengers and join the escalating gun game? Best of all, surely, to insist upon rigorous enforcement of the security checks – and that must apply to presidential security, too. The Bible teaches that while Christians should be harmless as doves, they should also be wise as serpents.

And such wisdom is now more necessary than ever with so many desperate minorities and individuals following suit. Wisdom suggests attending to *why* they become desperate in the first place, as well as how to forestall them. For this sort of evil is catching. It not only can happen here, it will happen here – it has happened here. And it seems to me a Christian duty to the innocent to stop it in its tracks, to make peace rather than to be passive.

Balanced Prayer

11 April 1981

Anyone who thought the Church of England was now entirely self-governing (if they had not been alerted by earlier events) must have stood corrected by Thursday evening's events in both houses of Parliament. The Lords by 28 votes to 17, and the Commons by 152 to 130, approved the introduction of the Prayer Book Protection Bill, under which an incumbent would be obliged to hold at least one service a month according to the rites of 1662 if petitioned to do so by twenty of his parishioners or more.

Clearly the Bill is aimed at the Alternative Service Book, with its modern English and (though few people ever mention this) its more generous churchmanship; for to speak of the ASB as if its language were the only difference is almost like criticizing a motorcar solely on the grounds of the colour it is painted. However, language – even literature – seems to be what the Prayer Book counter-reformation is concerned with. Some people have produced regional statistics to show that the new services have reduced the numbers attending church; but the official figures for the Church of England as a whole have gone up slightly since they were launched. Still, *post* is not necessarily *propter hoc*.

In the Commons, Lord Cranborne spoke of the slow murder of the Book of Common Prayer – one of the enriching glories of England. He denied that his Bill was a breach of the concordat under which the Church was promised the initiative in legislation affecting it; for had not the Archbishop of Canterbury himself promised that the

Prayer Book would only be touched by Parliament? It was the clergy who had broken the concordat. And in the Upper House, Lord Glenamara claimed that the clergy had had their arms twisted by the bishops until 1662 was relegated to the status of a rare antiquity and anyone who clung to it was branded an old-fashioned fuddy-duddy.

Back came the response: from Lord Hailsham (denounced by Lord Glenamara as appallingly biased) the assertion that grave questions of constitutional propriety were being raised; that the Bill was giving dictatorial powers to minorities; and that Cranmer's English could never be preserved by force of law. In the Commons, Mr Van Straubenzee was insisting that the Alternative Services were only alternatives, not substitutes, and that it was no longer fitting for a Parliament of today to concern itself with the domestic affairs of a Church which Parliament itself had equipped with its own Synod. The Book of Common Prayer was still entrenched in the laws of the land, but the fact was that the language of the sixteenth century no longer carried the same force. Well, as I've said, the Prayer Book supporters carried the day in both houses, but it seems most unlikely the Government will find them the time to go any further.

You must, of course, make up your own minds about it. At least the Church of England can't be accused of rushing things, for it's been experimenting – openly – with the new services for the past fifteen years. Indeed, they go back to a wartime request from the Chaplains to the Forces for a service book that servicemen could understand. It may also be worth noting that the Roman Catholics have modernized *their* language, and that the most vigorous of the Protestant evangelical churches – often the growing churches – use modern English too. Ah, BUT, on the other hand there *is* the glorious language, the literary gold-standard, the tradition. Let others do what they please, that is no reason why the Church of England should come down to their level. Do not many Catholics yearn for the Latin Mass?

One is trying hard to be balanced – which has lately become a fashionable word and is variously interpreted as meaning less exposure for views the hearer doesn't approve of, or ensuring that each side cancels the other out so that nothing is conveyed at all. Some people would rather that than trust others to disagree with what they hear. In the meantime, do the sacraments and Gospel reach the people, is the forgiveness of sins preached, does the Church serve the community – in any language?

The Humiliation of God

18 April 1981

For Christians this Easter Eve is the worst day in the year. And yet, it is almost the best. It is the worst because it is the day of abject defeat: the whole mission has been a mistake, a disaster, humiliated, stamped out and deterred for good. And yet this day is one of the best, because *we* know what comes next – the greatest comeback of all time, from total flop to utter triumph; not just victory in life, but victory over death. As I have said before, I don't know how it was done – I only know that something happened so powerful, so convincing, that for centuries it drove the Church forward to success, with the standard of failure – the cross – in its hand.

It hardly makes sense. The casualties were enormous. There were plenty of more attractive religions around. Neither the Jews nor the pagans were much impressed by the Jesus cult in its early days, and it won't do to say that it would never have got where it is today without the support of the Roman emperor: for how did it survive and grow until it forced itself upon Rome? I suggest the basic reason is to be found in the absurd claim that Jesus Lives. People knew it and still know it today, enough of them to give hope that the Church is still in its early days; that, as they say, it isn't that Christianity has failed but that it hasn't yet been tried – that it's still in its infancy. What right have we to expect its fullness in *our* time?

It is, in fact, an extremely adult religion. It will have nothing to do with childish notions that God can be manipulated by sacrifices, flattery and magic; or that God is so far above us that we can know nothing of him; or that we must be suffering now because of something we did in a former life. It teaches, right from the beginning of Genesis, that God created Man and Woman in his own image – which I take to mean Original Goodness – and then paid us the adult compliment of the freedom to choose to depart from that goodness. That is the simple, complicated, wonderful and horrifying answer to the tired old question: how can a loving and all-powerful God make such a hash of the world? The answer means he doesn't. We do; and if he didn't let us, we wouldn't be worth having, nor worth being. As for the all-powerful bit – I think the writer Philip Toynbee is heading in the right direction when he suggests that the only power God has is love. Love can be all-powerful, but only when it is responded to. Love without response is love unfinished; it needs response for its completion.

I have come to see lately that this matter of response is at the heart of faith. It is not enough for God, for Jesus, just to be or to die. At Easter, especially, what matters is our response – what difference it makes to us, how we change. I get the mad idea that the whole thing was set up to *shock* us into responding. 'So you won't listen to what I say? Then watch this! Down to the very depths – why have I forsaken myself? – God himself suffers defeat like the rest of us – then whoosh! Resurrection – the whole thing turned inside out.' As Hans Küng points out, Christ is not interested in success, he is showing us how to cope with failure.

Another mad idea: by suffering – indeed courting – death, Christ was saying to his disciples: 'You're never going to get anywhere hanging onto my earthly apron-strings. I shall have to remove my physical self in order to force you to discover the Christ within yourselves.' And that is what happened at Pentecost, with the discovery of the Holy Spirit. There are some who would say that in this way Christ has already returned – that the Second Coming has already happened. But I suppose others would call that heresy (though that's a word I have the utmost difficulty in getting even the most exalted churchmen to use nowadays).

Anyway, here comes Easter – an event which totally baffles every other religion, however respectful they may be of Jesus up to that point. The Koran, for instance, accepts the Virgin Birth and the Ascension, but insists that he was never killed or crucified. How it misses the point – that God's triumph is nothing without first God's defeat!

Troublesome Neighbours

25 April 1981

I get the feeling that we – well, some of us – are in danger of working ourselves up into a kind of hysteria, and I'm particularly worried about the part my own profession of journalism is playing in this. Every day in every way things seem to be getting worse and worse. Tension 'builds up', violence invariably 'erupts' (mindlessly), and everything proceeds from problem to crisis. Now I spend a good deal of time actually denying that journalism (alias 'the media') is responsible for all this. I still insist that journalists do not write the play – but they do greatly affect the acoustics of the theatre, and the lighting. And so I have a good deal of sympathy with the Archbishop of Canterbury when he complains that we are in danger of poisoning ourselves with bad news, although I think it is important to set this against the background of two considerations which profoundly affect the way journalism operates.

The first is that a bias towards good news would be just as disastrous, perhaps more so, than one towards bad news. In giving prominence to what is wrong with society, journalism is at least serving as an independent counterweight to a political establishment whose interest is to assert that everything's going splendidly. A 'Good News' press would soon be open to the charge of smugness and covering up. The media have to act as a warning system, or no one else will. The second consideration – not one, perhaps, of which the public ought to be aware all the time – is the sheer difficulty of practising journalism these days. Take television news: it is technically so complicated that it is something of a miracle to me that it gets on the air at all, let alone that it gets anything right. Time equals money, money equals time and we're short of both, so corners have to be cut, and sometimes by people who have not had the opportunity to immerse themselves very deeply in the situation. To cover a story like Brixton thoroughly would have required journalists living in the community – and living in the police force – for years. And, as I've said before, how can we publish the truth if those who know it won't tell it? But enough of journalistic whingeing.

What I would like to emerge from this is two more points, both of which have to do with loving our neighbour by listening to our neighbour – and hearing things we may not want to hear. The first point is that situations like Brixton or the H-blocks or the Civil Service strikes or the effect of unemployment on the Northwest or Cornwall (in both of which I have just been) are enormously complex, can only be understood from the inside, and are invariably embittered by efforts to explain them by simplifying from the outside (which is what most journalists, whether they like it or not, are required to do). Time and again, as a correspondent, I have walked into a situation that I have heard about or read about and found myself saying, 'But it's not like that at all.' And that is not because my colleagues have been distorting it, but because they have simply had to leave things out in order to fit times and spaces and budgets.

And the next point is what I can only call a matter of perspective. Every news story would have to be the length of *War and Peace* to give it its true significance against the national background.One just has to leave it to the public to look around them and realize that most young blacks are *not* rioting, most workers are *not* striking, most people in Northern Ireland are *not* interested in violence: in short, that the country is full of good, kind, orderly people (including blacks, policemen, trade unionists and Irishmen) despite the way many of them are mishandled – by superiors at the ends of their tethers.

If you seek this kingdom, look around you; not at the images on the TV screen but at your family and your parish, your literal neighbours. I've had three such insights this week: one a family wedding near Salisbury; the next a christening in a church near Land's End; the third in a small Lancashire town, where I was interviewing the vicar's wife. 'What does the Church mean to you?' I asked pompously, expecting some grandiose answer. 'It means St Bede's round the corner', she said. 'That's all I know and all I need to know.'

Scotch Broth

2 May 1981

This week I've been in Scotland. The BBC cupboard from which I have the privilege to address you now is in Edinburgh – surely the handsomest city in all these islands, though it would look better still if it washed more of the soot off its face.

I find it healthy to write occasional 'Yours Faithfullys' away from London; for one sees everything in a different perspective, including London itself. Up here it is sometimes quite hard to keep in touch with the wider world, owing to the tendency of the local broadcasting to spurn English offerings and put on something like a heresy trial on its hands. It appears that a certain minister of the Kirk, carried away by the experience of being 'born again', submitted himself to a second baptism at the hands of a pentecostal preacher who dunked him in the river. The scandal of this was not so much the style and nature of the second baptism, but the implication that the minister's original baptism as a Presbyterian infant was inadequate. I do not think that burning at the stake is still part of Scottish law, but – Gad, sir! – when is the Church of England going to take the Thirty-nine Articles as seriously? Only in Scotland do you meet calvinistic evangelicals who maintain that Jesus will *not* save all those who turn to him, but only those *predestined* to salvation. Some of us, you'll be worried to hear, are predestined to be damned – and I think that's in the Thirty-nine Articles, too, so Anglicans had better believe it.

Another thing that gives Scotland a special perspective is its family involvement with Northern Ireland. Many Glasgow Catholics have relatives in Ireland: some Glasgow Protestant families have migrated to Ulster and come back again. One Catholic priest told me that relations between them were now the best they had ever been, on the surface; but he was doubtful how deep they went. Like some other priests and ministers I met, he thought the Pope would do better to stay out of Glasgow next year, in the interests of ecumenism.

In areas like Clydebank, the Roman Catholic Church is deeply involved in the campaign against unemployment. But none of the Scottish churches seem to be bothered by critics calling upon them to 'stay out of politics'. Catholics and Protestants alike would think it an exceedingly odd view of Christian responsibility. 'The Kirk has always been involved in politicking and power', one of its departmental heads told me, and went on to describe how he and his colleagues had confronted a minister of the crown with the text 'Monetarism is an offence against God'. Anybody who imagines the Church of Scotland to be a pack of trendy lefties is standing language on its head. But it is also quite likely that this year the Kirk's assembly will vote for unilateral nuclear disarmament. That is not to say the Kirk is going pacifist all the way; but I think it has something to do with Scottish resentment at being used by the English war machine, something also to do with Scotland's missionary concern for the Third World.

I came across a rather sweet manifestation of this up in the ancient university town of St Andrews, where the Anglican bishop – Michael Hare-Duke – has arranged a Japanese-style Celebration of Peace for tomorrow (Sunday). It centres round a cherry tree, grown from a cutting from Nagasaki, and decorated with thousands of paper birds, folded in the Japanese origami tradition. There is (the Bishop tells me) an ancient Japanese custom of folding paper birds as if each was a prayer of hope; and anyone who folds a thousand birds will have their wish granted. There was, it seems, a little girl in Hiroshima, dying of radiation sickness, who began folding birds out of the wrapping papers her drugs came in, in the hope of being cured. She only got to 644 before she died, but ever since, people have sent paper birds to Hiroshima as prayers for peace. Well, tomorrow they'll be hanging from that cherry tree in St Andrews, and with them this prayer: 'Lead me from Death to Life, from Falsehood to Truth: Lead me from Despair to Hope, from Fear to Trust: Lead me from Hate to Love, from War to Peace: Let Peace fill our Heart, our World, Our Universe.'

Bobby Sands

9 May 1981

This is a piece I tried not to write, for it concerns the death of Bobby Sands, the IRA hunger-striker in Northern Ireland. It was an almost irresistible temptation to hold forth about him last week, but two things held me back. First, was it really a religious issue and not just a political stunt? And second, it's part of my philosophy of journalism that most stories are written too soon, before we are sure what has really happened or can put it into any kind of perspective wider than the hysteria of the moment.

Certainly it was a political stunt – among many other things. This is hardly the place to go into details, but I do think that if we believe ourselves to be on the side of the angels we have a special duty to think ahead and not allow the Devil to outmanoeuvre us, for example by allowing our prisons to become universities of disaffection. But if the Devil does force us into battle on ground of his own choosing, I think we have to confront him, and not run away on the excuse that we should not give him the publicity. If our cause is just, surely he should be exposed.

But is it really Angels against the Devil? The Christian has to acknowledge that there are sinful human beings, made in the image of God, on both sides. So that when the pack is howling damnation, somebody ought to make a deliberate – if distasteful – effort to look for the divine mixed up with the devilish.

And that, I think, has been at the centre of what the Roman Catholic Church has been up to in Northern Ireland. This Church – for all its recent efforts to condole with both sides – has taken a beating for not striking an unequivocal pose on the issue; and I must say I have met English and Scottish Catholic priests who cannot see how Mr Sands could legitimately have been given the last rites. But nowadays the Roman Church is almost as confused as the rest of us; its leaders are not immune to national points of view, nor (come to that) political possibilities; but it seems to me they are also reluctant to assume that they have the right to ignore the tiniest spark of the divine still burning in the blackest of sinners. For God has a way of choosing the most unattractive of individuals to pose his problems to us. And lest it be thought I am favouring one side, let us not overlook the amazing forbearance – in the face of murderous provocation – by Northern Ireland's Unionist majority. Secretly, most English people care little more for them than they do for Republicans; but here we come back to England's centuries-old failure to appreciate what Ireland (North and South) is like.

I spent much of last year helping to organize a series of Irish 'Thought for the Day' with that very failure in mind. The point was that it is futile to play word-games about the Irish from London if you do not appreciate the history, mythology, folk traditions and tribal solidarity that permeate Ireland. Far too few English journalists appreciate these. Goodness knows what the thirty or more foreign camera crews made of them, who descended upon Belfast for the last days of Bobby Sands. The Russians, I gather, gleefully discovered something called 'Human Rights'.

It is correct enough on one level to say Bobby Sands was a criminal who committed suicide to make trouble. But Republican Irish would say that deliberately ignores *their* level of meaning: that he was a patriot who gave his life for his country. He was, incidentally, the thirteenth Irish hunger-strike victim of this century, so with its overtones of famine and fasting (which Indians, too, hold meaningful) the act becomes rather more than mere suicide in Irish eyes. But if each side persists in sticking to its own level of meaning, we can only have the battle between devils, never the dialogue between sinners out of which alone reconciliation can come.

Let us try for a moment to escape the futile ping-pong of black and white. Christians have to seek a purpose in every disaster. If there could be anything redemptive in the death of Bobby Sands, only the living can bring it to life. But if it is fanned into death and more death, then it will have been a mere parody of martyrdom, and a blasphemy against sacrifice.

On Shooting the Pope

16 May 1981

There was a time, in the Middle Ages, when the Church made strenuous attempts to outlaw the crossbow and ban its use throughout Europe. It was seen as a weapon so terrible in its effects that no Christian should ever turn it against another. There was the additional blasphemy about it, that the crossbow was so powerful that its bolt – projected by a mere peasant – might pierce the armour of his social superior the mounted knight. And an exception was made for using it against Turks, infidels and other heretics. But I think the Church's basic instinct was absolutely right. In its heart of hearts it is moving in much the same direction against the nuclear bomb. But isn't it time Christians thought very seriously about their attitude towards a weapon far more widespread and practical – towards firearms in general and pistols (or 'handguns' as the

Americans call them) in particular? Yes, Christians especially should think about this, because it seems to me at least possible that one of the things God is trying to shout to us through the uproar over the shooting of the Pope (following the shooting of President Reagan, following the shooting of Martin Luther King, the Kennedy brothers and a host of others) is, 'What are you doing with those playthings of death? Throw them away!'

(By sheer coincidence, as I was writing those lines, I looked up and saw the windows across the street crowded with faces, peering out. The rumour was, 'There's a sniper on the roof!' It soon died down again, but nobody seemed surprised.)

The menace of the handgun has been with us long enough, Heaven knows: Queen Victoria was attacked with one, and a British Prime Minister (Spencer Perceval) was assassinated with one in 1812. But as the twentieth century moves towards its close, two important changes have taken place, in the quality and quantity of handguns. They have become more accurate, more devastating, with greater capacity and reliability; and there are far more of them about, cheap and easy to get. What is more, people's attitude towards them has changed. I do not want to blame this wholly on the Americans – their devotion to the handgun is fierce and deeply rooted in their history and social philosophy – but they do have a lot to answer for. The gun has become both a virility symbol and a guarantee that even the lowest of society's rejects can cut down the loftiest of society's heroes. I believe one gun was trade-marked 'The Equalizer'. When I lived in Washington, some of my neighbours were scandalized at my irresponsibility in not leaving my wife with a gun under her pillow to fight off rapists while I was away, and not having one in the car to beat off highway thugs. I have to say that with the police increasingly armed – and the criminal fraternity, too – it will not be long before a hankering after private pistols begins to spread on this side of the Atlantic, unless we stamp on it hard and now. And surely that must be a concern of the churches.

They are already concerned about the next level of fire-arms, the trade in rifles and machine-guns and, worse, in tanks and aircraft, which is usually justified with a mixture of 'jobs at any price' and 'if we don't sell jets to the Hottentots, somebody else will'. But just as the tiny legit-imate trade in pistols expands into an uncontrollable flood, so the official arms trade leaks into unofficial terrorist and guerrilla movements. There's a moral dilemma here, of course: are arms to be reserved exclusively to the already powerful and entrenched? In a sinful, fearful world, how can the oppressed free themselves if they are denied some-thing like equal force?

Well, if things have got that far, I doubt if there is any good way out, only bad ones. One can only pray for mercy on those who feel driven to take them. Wisdom must lie in not getting into situations which can only be changed by violent revolution.

Two Hundred Not Out

30 May 1981

There will be a modest 'Pop!' in our recording studio at the end of this talk, to mark the fact that this is the two hun-dredth 'Yours Faithfully' I've done. Actually, I should have known better than to say that, because it will only bring letters lecturing me on the evils of drink: of which, indeed, I'm only too well aware, though I would argue it brings a certain solidarity with those jolly sinners whose company Our Lord so much preferred to that of the righteous.

Every Friday afternoon, as for the past four years, a solemn – almost sacramental – procession moves through the corridors of Broadcasting House; down the lift to the Lower Ground Floor and into our decrepit studio L1 (known in the trade as 'The Boudoir'). The procession is headed by my diminutive secretary, Pam, bearing the sacred script and stopwatch, with me lumbering in the rear muttering about some doubtful phrase at the top of page two. One of our electronic wizards is waiting at the antique control panel, casting a spell over the equipment that will hold it together for just five minutes more – or rather, four minutes and forty seconds, in order to leave time for the announcer. Usually, we get it right first time although occasionally ten or fifteen seconds have to be cut out and thrown away to fit. Jokes and purple passages are the first to go. Then we listen through to it, and post the tape into the system which – so far – has always brought it onto the air next morning without fail.

There are usually three or four ideas for a 'Yours Faithfully' simmering in my head. Some are topical, others timeless; picked up from the news, from letters, conversations, daily life. 'Must do something about Hunger Strikes, about Feminine Spirituality, about Liturgical Dancing, about Heaven . . .' On Tuesday or Wednesday, one of these ideas is pulled forward onto the front burner and given a good stir while I'm walking my lethargic basset on Hampstead Heath. But I don't really know what it means until the paper goes into my typewriter on Friday morning and the words begin to appear before me at a pounding two-fingered pace. Sometimes they don't turn out to mean as much as I'd hoped. You can think you've got a thought until black-and-white reveals all too clearly that you haven't. I batter away for a couple of hours, with my back to the door and my face to a row of Bibles and dictionaries, pausing to make improvements with a bottle of correcting fluid and a little brush. Sometimes you'd think I was painting a picture, not writing a script.

Somewhere about now I begin to worry if I'm ever going to come to the point. Is this in any sense religious? I tell myself the whole of life is a religious experience; that all contemplation is prayer; but will that satisfy the people who write in demanding: 'Where was the Gospel last Saturday?' For these talks have made me acutely aware that broadcasting ought to be *two-way* communication. I'm doing this for the listener, and he or she writes back. I can't please all of them all the time: maybe I have to tell them things they would rather not hear. But there are polite ways of doing that. One should never insult the listener; though in the field of religion it is almost impossible not to tread on somebody's spiritual toes. It is arrogant to imagine one can be totally objective; and dishonest to dodge a conclusion if one can see it. But one should try to be fair.

I don't believe, you see (and I've said this before, but I'll say it again), that these little talks are as influential as some kind people suppose. What they do, on a good day, is to express what a fair proportion of listeners believe already but 'wish they could put it like that'. If only I could persuade those who write in to say I'm not fooling *them* that I'm not fooling the others, either; that the half million people who listen to these talks are as capable as anyone else of using their own critical faculties. None the less, if I do offend, I beg your forgiveness.

And so, on to our next hundred! I would like to think it could bring you comfort and joy. In the meantime, Yours Faithfully, Gerald Priestland.

Comfort and Joy

6 June 1981

I knew it! Last week's somewhat flippant reference to alcohol has brought me several smart raps across the knuckles, and even more for arguing that wine confers (and here I quote myself) 'a certain solidarity with those jolly sinners whose company Our Lord so much preferred to that of the righteous'. The righteous – insisting they were not *self*-righteous – did not like that at all. They wrote in accusing me of undermining the moral order by suggesting that sin did not matter, and of overlooking the crucial fact that Our Lord only mixed with sinners in order to call to repentance. I must say I do not get so stern a picture of him at all. He was very different from John the Baptist, for example. I think that, above all, he was calling on people to repent of hypocrisy, to be honest and open about themselves; for he loved them warts and all, and he wanted them to be fully human with a deep sense of joy.

Where can we find joy – comfort and joy – in this miserable world? Actually, all over the place, and I will give you four examples of where I have stumbled on it in the past couple of weeks.

Yesterday morning, driving to work, I saw a pretty girl standing at a zebra crossing, and I stopped for her. I always stop for blondes. (Sexist!) She hesitated. I spread my hands out and made a bowing gesture. She curtseyed – and trotted across. Pure innocent joy. Two human beings forgetting they were enemies called Motorist and Pedestrian and caring for one another.

There is joy in the Arts, too. Recently I was lucky

enough to see the musical *Cats*, and I have not enjoyed myself so much since (oddly enough) I first saw Wagner's *Götterdämmerung* – to which *Cats* has absolutely no resemblance. The only connection is that both were total experiences. A Christian could find a theme of Redemption in *Cats*, though frankly it is silly to look for much of a plot: *Cats* is really a choral ballet, and the joy of it lies in the flat-out service – the openness, too – that the audience gets from everyone: composer, designer, orchestra and above all those incredible singing dancers. It happens that I am a cat lover: but the choreographer has not fallen into the trap of making them do cute cat-imitations. If only we all worked so hard, so skilfully, and with such joy . . .

Or *ran* with such joy. You see that in a British film called *Chariots of Fire*, where the face of the actor playing the Scottish Olympic runner Liddell lights up with a holy joy as he bursts through to win. And holy it should be, for he was a dedicated servant of the Lord who refused to run on the Sabbath – the righteous can rejoice in that. As they should also in the victory of his Jewish colleague, Abrahams: for this is a film suffused with old-fashioned virtues like decency and brotherhood. I wonder if it may not convince other film-makers that it is, after all, possible to make a good and successful film without explicit sex and violence, and without making virtue seem ridiculous.

My last example comes from the experience of my wife. She is an artist, and teaches painting in various Old People's hospitals in London. One of the sad things about them is that so often the patients have nothing to do, nothing to stimulate their minds or to show for their time. Sometimes, when the resources can be found, my wife takes a class in wheelchairs to an Art Gallery; and the other day they went to the Tate. Turner was criticized for making his sea too rough and not having enough sails on his boats:

but everyone liked the Landseer dogs and Stubbs's horses, while Frith's 'Derby Day' was a topical success. One of the things they learned was that skies do not always have to be bright blue. On the way out they used the big sculpture lift to take the wheelchairs, and one of the old folk complained it was going down very slowly. My wife explained it was meant for moving statues, which could be very fragile. At which the lift operator spoke up: 'But we've got something more valuable in here', he said. 'We've got life.'

All We Like Toads

13 June 1981

There have been continued protests from the respectable at my suggestion that Jesus actually preferred the company of sinners – including a splendid letter from a former Moderator of the Kirk Assembly tainting me with Antinomianism (than which, as you will know, there is no graver heresy). I tried to answer that last week, and if we do not see eye to eye, we do not see eye to eye. I did not, incidentally, say that Jesus preferred criminals, perverts and rapists, as some listeners thought; and I cannot believe that, say, football hooligans would seek to justify their behaviour by saying 'But Jesus loves me'. Let us not leap to nonsensical conclusions, dear listener in Staffordshire.

I earned reproach from another quarter for citing, last week, several instances of joy all derived from *earthly* pleasure. (This is not unconnected.) Well, as I understand it, all our experience of grace has to be mediated to us by something here on earth, though I suppose that is a somewhat Catholic way of putting it.

Let us continue to enjoy ourselves. Let me offer you, at

about fourth hand, quite the most enjoyable item of news to come my way during the past week. I got it from Libby Purves, who got it from *The Times*, which got it ultimately from Dr L. Fairchild, a zoologist of Duke University in North Carolina; and it concerns toads.

The female toad, unaware of spiritual values, likes her mate big. But because she normally pairs in the dark, she has only one way of judging: the bigger the toad, the deeper his croak. However, there is a complicating factor, because a cold toad gives a deeper croak. Male toads therefore cunningly make for the coldest corner of the pond to deepen their croaks; and a female who thinks she is mating with a large, warm toad may in fact have been deceived by a small, cold one.

However, things do not stop there. Since all the toads are trying to chill off as much as possible, the large ones tend to win in the end and take over the cold spot. Indeed, says Dr Fairchild, many of the smallest toads are forced right out of the pond and are obliged to sit on the bank where (since it is warmer out of the water than in it, even in North Carolina) the small toads' croaking becomes even shriller and less enticing. However, there is still the chance of consolation for the warm weaklings. For in order to get into the pond, females do, of course, have to run the gauntlet of the bank; where, says Dr Fairchild, the small males make the most of their opportunities . . . It should not be long before the large toads learn to lurk on the bank and shut up.

This week's problem is how to get a sermon out of all this, since surely it must mediate something. The Bible is not much help, since I find no reference to toads in it – only frogs. One might give the story the old analogy twist, and say: 'Dear friends, how very like toads we are, aren't we? Skirmishing to win the best place in the pond, in the hope that our position will impress people, that the authority in our voice will win us a prize we do not strictly merit. And often we get away with it – because we are all of us croaking in the dark. Unlike the Supreme Being, who knows how small and insignificant we are and who is not impressed by our hypocritical cries, we deceive each other and are in turn deceived. Some of us even drop out of the struggle that is set before us, and try to grab what we have not earned, even though it is more obvious than ever that we have not earned it. That is what the so-called Permissive Society is all about. When are we going to learn that the Creator has destined a proper voice and a proper place for each one of us? Yet all we, like toads, have gone astray . . .'

In my time, I have heard more far-fetched sermons than that, including a most involved one explaining conversion in terms of cheese-making. For myself, I can only say that Creation is not just solemn and wonderful, but hilarious. It is another case of joy, I suppose; joy in the ingenuity of those lowly and disgraceful toads.

Signs From Heaven

20 June 1981

I still have my great-grandfather's prayerbook from the days when my ancestors lived in the Isle of Man. It was supplied by the Society for Promoting Christian Knowledge through something quaintly called Mank's Fund; and it contains all kinds of special prayers calling on God to assuage the malice of our enemies and confound their devices, or alternatively blessing His Holy Name for appeasing the seditious tumults which have lately been raised amongst us; prayers which one might have thought would come in handy today, but which seem to be missing from the Alternative Service Book, for all its comprehensiveness. According to its index, the ASB has prayers for Abbots and Angels, prayers for Social Responsibility and Synods, for Victory of a purely spiritual kind, and for Vocation. But the vigorous old service of Commination has gone – with its 'Cursed are the unmerciful, fornicators and adulterers, covetous persons, idolators, slanderers, drunkards and extortioners' – so has (long since) that service of thanksgiving for the exposure of the gunpowder plot. Curiously, the Alternative Service Book seems to have given up all hope of influencing the weather.

Great-grandfather's prayerbook (indeed, even my own edition of the 1662) has us humbly beseeching moderate rain and showers, or acknowledging our desert of 'a plague of rain and waters'; or, on the other hand, giving humble thanks for the refreshment of joyful rain or (alternatively) for 'this seasonable and blessed change of weather'. But it has all gone now – either because the Church has learnt from experience there is nothing it or God can do about the weather, or because nowadays we are too scientifically enlightened to hold with supernatural tinkerings. Instead of miracles, we talk of providence.

I have known some very pious weather forecasters – and any number of religious scientists. Few members of the scientific community claim that science will ever be final, or free of metaphysical assumptions; so there will always be room for religion, even though it, too, has to acknowledge it does not know the final answers. But to divorce it from the weather – which must have been man's very first reason for realizing he depended on some higher influence – seems to me a pity.

The Bible, of course, teaches otherwise. Long before Moses went up Sinai to conclude Israel's covenant with Jehovah, God had concluded his treaty with Noah and sealed it with a rainbow; and thoroughly meteorological that contract was (read Genesis, chapter nine). All through the Old Testament, the Lord sends floods and storms and 'fair weather cometh out of the North: with God is terrible majesty'. Jesus bade the storm to cease – though there are those who say he knew perfectly well that those Galilean lake-squalls blew themselves out soon; and I am told the alleged vagueness of our own weather forecasting is due not to the capriciousness of the Almighty, but to the difficulty of knowing exactly what is going on over the surrounding seas.

We should be grateful for what we get. Having spent part of my working life trying to escape excessive heat in places like Iraq, and intolerable cold in Canada, I think a temperate climate which seldom goes too far either way is a blessing. Praying about the weather should not be a matter of lobbying God to bend the rules, but, as always, an opportunity for acknowledging we are part of his creation and trying to hear his explanation of our role in it. Give thanks, by all means – we do not do enough of that; and I do not see anything wrong with the occasional sincere protest, if we are prepared to hear his side of the case as well. But the Alternative Service Book is probably right in trying to lead us away from an idolatrous view of God the Cosmic Conjurer towards the God of Love who wills us to look into every situation and see how we can care for one another. Jesus, you will remember, was contemptuous of people who reckoned they could read the sky and tell if it was going to be foul or fair tomorrow – but who could not discern the signs of the times and hear the voice of the prophet.

Holy Conversation

27 June 1981

If the last few talks in this series have sounded rather detached from the news, let me offer an explanation – and slip in a bit of sly publicity at the same time. The fact is, I am spending six days a week (*not* the Sabbath, please note) writing a book for the BBC; a book which will ultimately take the air next autumn in the form of a series to be called (I blush to say) 'Priestland's Progress'. Whether Priestland will actually make any spiritual progress remains to be seen; but the idea is of a plain man's pilgrimage through the main features of the Christian faith, with some comments, incidentally, from Jewish and Muslim friends. It is a full-time job, which is why I have not been out and about among the church assemblies and other exciting events.

However, I still read the papers; and I see there is a new issue of *Debrett's Etiquette and Modern Manners* to guide hostesses of country house parties. I have no evidence later than the works of P.G. Wodehouse and Agatha Christie that anyone does give country house parties any more – since they have never asked me to one – but if they do, it seems that it is now positively bad form to query the morals of young unmarried people who are patently living together, by giving them separate bedrooms. Not only must this be a relief to hostesses who have not got enough rooms: it accords with the consensus of the moral theologians I have been interviewing for my book, most of whom treated the phrase 'living in sin' as if it were a survival from the Venerable Bede. Formality and stuffiness are to be swept away, according to the guide's editor.

More valuable from my own point of view is the news that it is now OK to air three hitherto forbidden topics of dinner table conversation: illness, politics and religion.

I must say I regret the release of the first: when illness is not positively embarrassing, there is nothing more open to one-upmanship than playing 'more cardiovascular than thou' by rolling multicoloured capsules over the tablecloth. Politics and religion were presumably outlawed for causing friction – no hostess wants half her guests not talking to the other half – so I suppose it's a sign of slow maturity among our upper classes that they can now be trusted to talk about these matters without coming to blows. I hope, however, that when it comes to politics there will be no nonsense about 'What really matters is policies, not personalities'. Everyone knows that policies eventually collapse, leaving us with nothing but personality to rely on. Indeed, it could be argued that it is choosing the wrong personalities that causes the policies to collapse.

And personality – the personality of God, the personality of Jesus – is surely at the root of the Christian religion. I would go to a country house party in a flash if I thought there was going to be some good religious conversation, instead of gossip about horses, motorcars and tax avoidance. They say that in Old Constantinople, every baker's boy could discuss the Arian heresy; while in mid-seventeenth-century England, every tavern was a hotbed of radical theology. I suspect the ban on country house religion may have had something to do with not wishing to embarrass recusant Catholic landowners, whose affiliations were strictly illegal. We do not have to worry about that today; and some of the most stimulating religious conversations I have had lately have been with Jewish friends.

But somehow I do not think religion will take the place of

the weather or that other appalling staple of conversation. last night's television programme on granny-bashing or the cancer-causing properties of lettuce (programmes I have always missed). The fact is, too few people know enough about their religion to be able to talk about it. They say they know what they believe, but if they tried talking about it, they might find they did not. Also, words like 'God', 'Love' and 'Jesus' are considered ungrown-up, or only suitable for church. Which is jolly odd, and a very good reason for doing two things: finding out what the faith really is about, and then talking about it. It makes a change.

Folk Religion

4 July 1981

Before I really get going, a correction and an apology: last week, tossing out a frivolous example of the kind of television programme everyone's been watching but me, I conjured up one on 'the cancer-causing properties of lettuce'. One listener took me seriously and another, a lettuce-grower, didn't, but was afraid I would damage his trade. Let me say here and now that I am assured lettuce does *not* cause cancer. I only chose it because it seemed so unbelievable. Carry on munching.

But, in a way, it does show that some people will believe almost anything. Deep down inside the British people there is a yearning to believe which some of my clergy friends refer to as 'Folk Religion'. Clergymen regard it with uncomfortably mixed feelings, because while much of it is profoundly unChristian, it does provide the basis on which a great deal of church life is built.

One eminent bishop told me he felt very ambivalent

about it. 'On the one hand,' he said, 'I'm very much aware that it looks in the opposite direction to Christian truth over so many things; yet I can't dismiss or despise it, because in many ways it is the only form in which people's instinct for God finds expression. Where the puritanism of the Church dismisses Folk Religion, we are probably doing more harm than good.'

But what is Folk Religion? Well, there's a vestigial belief in God as something rather more than Fate: Fate-with-a-personal-pronoun, if you will. Quite a lot of prayer goes on, especially at times of crisis. And a lot more people read the Bible than ever go to church. Much of Folk Religion has to do with our fear of death and our desire for some sort of continuing relationship with people we have loved. Taking flowers to a grave and visiting cemeteries is part of it. The Bishop thinks that the necessary increase in cremations rather than interment is bound to have an insidious effect on our Folk Religion; and so is the secularization of our public holidays, like Whitsun. That's cutting people off at their tap-roots. So is the gradual conversion of Christmas from a winter festival of family reunion into a TV-watching marathon.

There's a book by Bruce Reed, called *The Dynamics of Religion*, which has some interesting points to make about it. It gives the typical example of a village church which nobody uses, and yet when it's threatened with closure, there's a great uproar and everyone rallies round and raises the money to put it in good repair. It's the church *building* they worship, not what it stands for: or perhaps they make it stand for something quite other than its real purpose. Or again, there are the mothers who don't go to church but insist on the vicar baptizing their babies. They simply haven't grasped the Christian meaning of the symbols: there's dysfunction, disconnection between the symbol and the thing symbolized. The symbol gets worshipped for itself; magical powers are attributed to it, and immense importance is attached to 'doing things right'. Reed claims that this inability to grasp the inner meaning leads to fundamentalism – to expectations that biblical and liturgical language, or the doctrines of the church leader, will literally describe what happens. In short, it leads to magical idolatry. Things that the Church regards as on the fringe get moved to the centre; things at the heart of the Christian faith are banished to the fringe, uncomprehended.

Some of this goes back to pre-Christian Folk Religion. Many churches were built on the site of pagan temples which did seek to manipulate the god, and regarded religion as going from us to him. But the essence of Christianity is that it comes from him to us, and most of what goes on in church is *not* meant to be us doing things for him – not holy good works – but the signs of what he does for us: grace, redemption, forgiveness, the sacraments of various kinds, and the Gospel of hope. Christianity really is different in this way: it is a very sophisticated reversal of Folk Religion. But without instruction, few people realize this. In our bones, we still think it's magic.

Life's a Riot

11 July 1981

It's a coincidence, of course, that this year marks the fifth centenary of the Peasants' Revolt; a coincidence, but a meaningful one. For the rioters in our streets – and one can't say often enough that they aren't only black, by any means – are the new peasantry, the despised bottom of the heap. Once you despise people enough and give them the impression they are regarded as beasts, what have they got to lose? All over the world you can see it: they'll behave like beasts.

But that is not the whole story. Everyone has had their say about the recent disturbances – I'm afraid I am jumping onto an already crowded bandwaggon – but one of the most sensible comments I have heard came from Mr Len Murray of the TUC, observing that it wasn't good enough to blame them on the government, the blacks, the police or the young: everyone was involved – all of us have failed to some degree. Complex events never have simple causes, and when a whole society starts breaking down, everyone needs to examine their conscience. It is not very uplifting to hear our elected representatives blaming each other, as if this society had only been founded two years ago, or as if everything that happened could be traced directly and solely to some official action. The question has already been raised as to whether the adversary system of politics – 'I'm totally right – you're totally wrong' – is democratically effective; it might also be considered whether it is Christian. The Gospel teaches that we are *all* sinners; even politicians and, yes, even broadcasters.

So far as I can make out, the churches have a little less to be ashamed of than most bodies; and I am not thinking only of the clergy who have been out in the streets, at no little risk, trying to calm things down, nor of the united leadership – Roman Catholic, Anglican and nonconformist – offered by the prelates of Merseyside. I am thinking of the prophetic warnings that have been published for years past by men like Archbishop Derek Worlock and Bishop David Sheppard. It must have been at least three years ago that Bishop Sheppard made the General Synod cringe with his denunciation of the way this country had built Liverpool up as a great trading centre and then turned its back upon it. And it was almost five years ago that Bishop Hugh

Montefiore launched his warning of the nation's approaching Apocalypse. I have a fistful of pamphlets from all over the churches about the strains upon our society imposed by racialism, unemployment, inner city devastation and the battering of the family. They read now like the prophecies of Cassandra: truth that nobody would believe. It is the shame of the churches that while they saw the truth, they were held in such low esteem that nobody heeded them. At best they were told to keep their noses out of matters they did not understand.

Which is not to excuse the rioters as innocent pawns of the system: nobody need be that. But everybody needs some purpose in life by which he can respect himself, and neither Church nor State has been able to supply a worthwhile 'purpose' for the street gangs. To a frightening extent, we are becoming a purposeless society, and against that background rioting and looting are simply rather fun – a way of insulting the helpless affluence that tries to go its way without you. Another appalling feature is that so much of the violence is being committed by children: neither parent nor church nor school has anything to be proud of in that. The police – who have suffered unbelievable provocation, whatever their shortcomings – are not supposed to take over *their* functions. Had this been the United States, we would have had shooting in the streets, and a body-count in the news bulletin every morning.

Things will calm down eventually given good humour – they always do – and the temptation will be to pretend it never happened and that our society is all right really, that all it needs is better riot equipment, longer prison sentences or some short, sharp shocks. I should like to quote my old friend, the Abbé de Tourville: 'Things go wrong in order to show us it is God's will that we should change them. He keeps the world moving in order to shake us out of our old set shapes.'

Wesley's Bishops

18 July 1981

Some years ago, when I was in Hawaii, a taxi driver said to me – with great reverence – 'Sir, I wish to thank your country for the gift of John Wesley.' (Hawaii, incidentally, still incorporates the Union Jack in its state flag.) Well, last week, Wesley's church here in Britain made a gift to our religious life which I think would have gladdened the heart of its founder. Its conference, meeting in Norwich, voted by a crashing 497 voices to 5 to approve the Covenant for Unity with the Church of England, the United Reformed, the Moravians and the Churches of Christ; and one far-reaching implication of that, with its mutual recognition of membership and ministry, is that the Methodists will eventually appoint bishops. They will not (it was emphasized) be re-ordained, and they will remain sober superintendents at heart, rather than princely prelates 'all gas and gaiters'. As a matter of fact, I don't know any gaseous prelates in the Anglican Church, either; and their stipends hardly allow for princely living. But the very gesture of Methodism moving 'up market', as it were, to episcopacy is both generous and historic.

Wesley himself struggled hard to keep Methodism within the Church of England. It was not by his choice that it was shut out. Not long ago that eminent Methodist, Lord Soper, said to me, 'I don't think I was ever a member of a divided church. For me, Methodism is a preaching order within the Holy Catholic Church, and I wish it would get back to that.' Wesley's movement was meant to be a *society* within the greater Church – somewhat as there are religious societies within Roman Catholicism – and it may well be that this kind of diversity is what we shall get under the Covenant. But what about the bishops?

To Anglicans – especially Anglican Catholics – the episcopacy is the essential link with that continuous Church that stretches back to the apostles, and demonstrates that Anglicanism is not an invention out of the blue but truly the Church Catholic in England. Bishops are the shepherds of their clergy, just as the clergy are the shepherds of their lay people. They are also the guardians of sound doctrine – and there's a hint here that religious truth is not to be determined by majority votes in assemblies. It is this kind of authority (not much exercised today, it has to be said) that has made congregationally-minded people suspicious of them; and the abandonment of that suspicion says a great deal for Methodist charity. It also says that Methodist leadership was under some pressure from congregations which were already engaged in local ecumenical schemes and were liable to go it alone if their leaders did not go with them.

John Wesley himself believed that the three-fold order of deacons, priests and bishops was scriptural and normal but not invariable. He came to believe that the claim to an uninterrupted succession of bishops descending from the apostles was 'a fable'. Nevertheless, in a desperate attempt to secure proper ordination for his men so that they could administer sacraments, early Methodists resorted to Irish and Scottish bishops – even to a bogus Greek Orthodox – until a study of the early Church of Alexandria suggested that it was all right for presbyters to ordain bishops, who could in turn ordain more presbyters. There is a good deal of room for argument here, and I have seen it written that Wesley 'regarded himself as a sort of bishop'. The essential point is, however, that one can't really maintain that episcopacy is alien to the spirit of Wesley. Several overseas Methodist churches have bishops, although of course they do not have quite the same overtones as they do in England, where the established Church has its seats in the House of Lords – surely something which will now have to be thought through anew.

In his presidential address to this year's Methodist Conference, Dr John Newton had this to say (which I think applies not only to Methodists): 'The Church is not called to be a ghetto, but an open house for humanity. Are we a Comprehensive School of Christ, open to all sorts and conditions of men? Or a selective entry, fee-paying establishment, patronized chiefly by the middle classes?'

Not The Royal Wedding

25 July 1981

One of these days there will be a programme entitled '*Not* the Royal Wedding'; but this isn't it. After all, the marriage of the Prince of Wales to Lady Diana is focused upon a religious ceremony, and if we are celebrating with a national party, I can't see any reason not to join in. Most of us could do with a good party after what we've been through lately, and I think the media owe the public a little light relief.

Not – as the service will remind us – that the honourable estate is to be taken in hand lightly (and more of that in a moment); but there is good biblical precedent for some feasting to help launch it. I'm thinking, of course, of the marriage in Cana of Galilee, where Jesus turned the water into wine – though I think it was Dorothy Sayers who suggested that what he really did was to catch the caterers smuggling out some real wine in water pots, and gave them the chance to put it back without losing face. Be that as it may, merry-making wasn't boycotted by Our Lord, even in his grim times. And though he did not himself marry (celibacy being no less honourable in Christian eyes; indeed, sometimes more so), none the less marriage becomes a powerful image in Jesus's teaching.

The Church, however, has had a good deal of trouble making up its mind about it. Could something that was apparently part social, part carnal and part financial really be a sacrament of grace – especially when the bride and groom appear to be acting as ministers to each other, with the priest as little more than a witness? It was not until the tenth century that the Church really took over marriage as its monopoly. There must be many people who find it hard to see matrimony as 'signifying the mystical union betwixt Christ and his Church' today; and fewer still who regard it as breakable only by death. The Church of England – which has long taken the strictest of views against remarriage of the divorced – has just agreed, in principle, to relax them. We have even seen an Anglican bishop marrying a divorced lady at a Baptist church in Wales. Scandalous? Well, I think we should pay attention to what he has to say. Divorce, says the Bishop, is Hell – as those who have experienced it know. But in Hell, God can still forgive us; he sets us free to make a new start. And this good news of repentance and forgiveness is the rock-truth of Jesus, on which he builds our homes, and through which day by day God recreates our marriages.

A sombre turn of thought on such an occasion. But I don't think it is unChristian to suggest that at the joyful start of a new marriage, we should be slow to condemn those who have tried and failed; and *very* slow to assume that their failure has been light and frivolous or without intense suffering and grief. Perhaps we should remember and pray for them, too.

But, as the poet Spenser writes in his *Prothalamion*, 'Ah, here fits not well Old woes but joyes to tell, Against the bridale day, which is not long: Sweete Themmes runne softly, till I end my song.' There are, of course, new woes as well as old ones: people complaining that the money could better be spent on the poor and the unemployed, or demanding to know why the country should be brought to a standstill for a couple of wealthy aristocrats with more privileges than you've had hot dinners. I must say, it's not a way of life I should care for, though I almost made a monarchist of a Russian journalist who once asked me if our Queen was *very tyrannical*: if you must have a Head of State, and people to go round opening and inspecting things and shaking hands (and every country does require such people), then surely it's best to have it done in style by dedicated professionals – which is what we have. Actually, I suspect we have a good deal more: a kind of spiritual last reserve, too; but like all reserves, you can only draw out of it what you put in.

We are, of course, free to legislate ourselves into a secular republic, though I doubt if it would be much of a vote-getter. In the meantime it's to be hoped that Wednesday's wedding will give to the royal couple quite as much as the pleasure we shall get.

Truro in London

1 August 1981

The British may not be much good at the bread these days, but they can certainly manage the circuses. That was about the only cynical comment I heard on the Royal Wedding, which surely was the great thing about it: a day free of cynicism, which everyone could take at its own high valuation of itself. If I must pick out one perfection from it, then it was Mr Speaker Thomas's lesson in how to speak, as he read from St Paul.

But London has another great event this week in the arrival of its new bishop, Dr Graham Leonard, from Truro. And as luck has it, this week also sees the publication of his new book *God Alive*, actually a series of lectures in Pastoral Theology, dedicated to the parish priests of Cornwall. It should give his new flock in London some idea of the kind of overseer it has acquired.

Dr Leonard finds in the modern Church many of the problems that disturbed St Paul in Corinth, including Gnosticism, Antinomianism, and a lack of authority and marriage discipline. 'The Church today', he laments, 'shows at times an almost pathetic desire to be loved by the world. She is happy, in T.S. Eliot's words, to dream of systems so perfect that no one will need to be good.'

There follows an interesting analysis of our multi-racial, multi-cultural society which Dr Leonard holds partly responsible for the public irrelevance of religion. But he blames also our 'impatience with time as necessary for growth . . . the search for happiness based on the satisfaction of immediate desires rather than the attainment of excellence through discipline and sacrifice'. Dr Leonard teaches flatly 'A desire for immediacy is incompatible with the development of spiritual or moral goodness'; and he goes on to argue that whereas the rewards of evil are paid on the spot, the transactions of good are generally on a long-term credit basis. 'The desire to achieve satisfaction without cost', he writes, 'is closely related to another feature of the present moral climate: the refusal of people to accept responsibility for their actions.' Further, 'while personal responsibility is in decline, moral indignation is on the increase', though on a highly selective, sentimental and long-range basis. It is also assumed – contrary to what St Paul teaches about the distinct roles of the different parts of the body – that if people are equal, they must be interchangeable. The Bishop ends his analysis by denouncing the vices of Envy and Greed. It might be stimulating to hear him in debate with a professional body of advertisers.

How should Dr Leonard's priests tackle such a world? Always, sacrifice and discipline are the key words. They must eschew the attitude that suffering is the worst evil, and that anything is justified that appears to relieve suffering. For, says Dr Leonard, 'this is a bent world . . . and whenever love comes face to face with evil, love will suffer. Not to suffer is not to love.' And the Bishop argues that if we try to avoid suffering, we will cut ourselves off from real contact with our fellow men and women and, in the end, learn nothing from life. This I find very compelling. Some of the best minds in the Church are now focused upon this connection between suffering and love. Dr Leonard says the only way for the Christian to deal with suffering and evil is to deny it any response save to let it spend its force within us and exchange it for 'that which is of God'.

The Christian, then, must recover a sense of discipline and sacrifice; and, according to Dr Leonard, this is where his priest comes in. He must push the Christian beyond what comes easily to him. He must give specific instruction not only in the faith but on *how* to worship, *how* to pray, *how* to receive the sacraments and use the Bible. His worship must be specifically Trinitarian, his Eucharist fully catholic, his prayers might be aided by the rosary. If Dr Leonard gets his way, there's going to be a lot less humanism and do-it-yourself Christianity in the pews of London, and vicars had better brush up their Trinity.

Notes and Queries

8 August 1981

Let it not be said this notebook is one-sided. The other day I received, from a listener in the West of England, what is in every sense a stiff letter denouncing the theory 'that we are all to blame for the recent riots', a statement which my correspondent damns as 'fatuous'. He goes on:

'After fifty years of trying to live a reasonably decent, law-abiding existence without wittingly harming any of my fellow creatures, I feel no more to blame for these explosions of criminality in our cities than I do for the slave trade or the troubles in Northern Ireland, and I am sick and tired of being told otherwise.'

Having dismissed one sweeping generalization, my West of England listener launches another of his own: 'What we are witnessing now is the logical outcome of thirty years' decline in moral leadership and example, during which time the country's leaders in government, education, management, unions and religion have stood aside wringing their hands and abdicating all responsibility as they retreated before the tide of greed, self-gratification, brutishness and loony liberality which has washed unchallenged – except by a brave and much-reviled few – over this once fair land.'

Well, it is nice to know there is somebody (indeed there are probably millions) satisfied they have done their social duty more than adequately over the past half century, and whose consciences are entirely clean. Harder to understand, though, why they haven't carried those feckless leaders with them – if, indeed, it is true that those leaders have done nothing but wring their hands. Could it be that my listener is wringing his? That he could have done more than keep the law and do no harm? He sounds like just the person to give leadership and assume responsibility himself. If he had, things might have been otherwise: if we all had . . .

One of the most pointed observations I heard during the week came from a lady who rang up a London 'phone-in show to pay special tribute to the music turner-over to the organist of St Paul's. 'After all', observed the lady, 'she was the only woman apart from the bride to have any function in the Royal Wedding.' If you omit, too, the chief bridesmaid and that joyous singer, Kiri Te Kanawa, I think a point has been scored there.

I'd like to use the rest of my time to answer the mounting queries: 'What about Priestland's Progress?' This doesn't mean my health or my holidays: it's the title of the series we shall be launching on 20 September as a kind of Plain Man's Guide to the Fundamentals of the Christian Faith.

It struck us that many believers – myself included – have only the vaguest home-made ideas of what Christianity is really about. In theory, people have learnt it in church or at school or at their mother's knees – but in practice, it is less and less true. And so – on the basis of 'If we don't do it, who will?' – Priestland is to be pushed out, map in hand and tape-recorder on his back, to enquire the way of those he meets on the road.

Bombs and Babies

15 August 1981

If this is the Silly Season, I tremble to imagine what it will be like when things get serious. For I can think of at least four moral issues in the air at present, any one of which must give the religious-minded person pause for thought.

One literally in the air is yet another of those traffic controllers' strikes. I happen to be a trade unionist myself, but surely – if you're a public servant – it is wrong to victimize the hapless holiday-maker as a way of getting your demands, especially if you expect not to suffer the consequences of your actions while others do. But on the other hand, the American example does seem to prove that their system of oaths and enforceable contracts isn't necessarily any better than ours. So that the real issue goes further back still: how to combine the interests of public, management and employees, and yet not pretend that human nature is without flaw and that disputes can be entirely eliminated. There would be something inhuman in a society without disputes; as there already is in one which allows the innocent to suffer.

The suffering of the innocent lay at the heart of the argument over the mongol baby whose parents wanted her to die, and who was taken over by the court and kept alive. It seems to me here that – since we cannot know how things are going to turn out – everyone can claim to be doing right as they see it. The parents and their doctors were ready to do – no doubt in the greatest agony of conscience – what is discreetly done every day: 'Thou shalt not kill, but needst not strive officiously to keep alive.' But once the case was in public hands, neither the local authority nor the Court of Appeal could have acted otherwise than they did – which was to give the child every opportunity to live. I read one letter in *The Times* which said the court 'has condemned the baby to a helpless life, and the parents to a living death'. Well, I wonder. I know a twenty-year-old mongol girl of whom that is totally untrue, and even if it were to prove true of the one in question, it would only show, I think, that hard cases make bad law – indeed, that making law on these things, relieving people of their moral dilemmas, is a poor way to go about it. If the State is to preserve all babies at all costs, it may have to look after them and pay for them. If it is going to get into the business of who is going to live – why not who's going to die, of what, and when? Tinkering with free will, and the personal responsibility that comes with it, must have its limits if right and wrong are not to become merely legal and illegal.

Innocence is hardly the word to apply to the H-block hunger-strikers. A cynic suggested to me the other day that the best way of ending their fasts would be for the British government to let it be known it welcomed the self-elimination of trouble-makers. But that would be barbarous, and it is sometimes forgotten that one reason hunger-strikers die is that the prison authorities are no longer prepared to employ the barbarous (and sometimes fatal) method of force-feeding. Everyone who has attempted to mediate seems to have retired with burnt fingers; but surely no Christian can rest happy with the thought of human life being squandered – either voluntarily or, at the gunman's hand, involuntarily. To protest our innocence of all this doesn't make it go away.

Nor, it seems, does the Bomb go away: and it's back in the new improved form of the Neutron Bomb. This would appear to be marginally less horrible than the dirty old

H-Bomb, but this is hardly the place to argue technical merits. The Russians will have it soon enough, if they haven't got it already, and the balance of terror will simply have become more expensive, at a time when the world has better things to do with its time and money. The fact that I am personally a pacifist does not prevent me from seeing the arguments of the military men – who have, so far, managed to avert the war we so much dread. The peace movement seems to be growing in popularity, but it still has to confront certain grave weaknesses: notably, its inability to grow spontaneously behind the Iron Curtain, and its difficulty in explaining how it would deal, practically, with human wickedness.

The Sea, The Sea

22 August 1981

Like a good many people on holiday, I have been contemplating the sea. Never having been in outer space, it is the most mysterious thing I know. One is never quite at home with it, and I have a sneaking primitive feeling – which experience sailors may challenge, but I think most landsmen share – that God's writ does not entirely run at sea. I don't say it's the Devil's but I think the sea is its own master. Jesus walked on it, you may say, and commanded it to be still. Yes, but that was a lake, really; he'd have had a much tougher time with the Atlantic. And there's that eerie passage at the beginning of Genesis: 'Darkness was upon the face of the deep. And the Spirit of God moved upon the face of the waters . . .' It is as if the sea were there already, waiting for him. Not very sound theology, perhaps, but from something within us.

The Psalms do have their great bursts of nautical gusto; but in general, the Bible wishes there were *no more sea.* I can't think of a single great religion which cares much for it. Judaism, like Islam, came out of the desert. Buddhism, like Hinduism, out of the forests and river-banks. Even mountains are more accommodating. Religion only comes to terms with the sea through islands; it is full of holy islands which conjure up an atmosphere of Good besieged by Evil and defying it. It is just as well that the human lifespan is so short; because if we could condense time, we would be aware that the sea is always winning, that the islands are being gnawed away and falling down. The holiest of islands will eventually end up under the water, and there will be more legends of church bells tolling in the deep.

The simple facts are, I suppose, that we are land creatures and that although we can devastate the earth with our bombs and bulldozers, there is very little we can do, even now, to control the colossal energies of the sea. Our seaside holidays are more side than sea; our bathing more in the sun (if we can find it) than surf. The sea is there to provide the fresh air and the feeling of spaciousness. Contemplating it for too long produces a sense of unease. The continuous rustling that you hear from a clifftop has a numbing effect upon the mind: I don't find it at all a good place for prayer (for I like my prayer to be human) and what I get from the sea is a kind of oriental absorption into the infinite – an obliteration of the self. Maybe I ought to let go and let it happen, but I daren't. There's even a hint of self-annihilation about it: come and drown yourself in me, it seems to be saying. No, thank you.

But of course there was a whole race of jolly Celtic saints who revelled in the sea. St Azenor of Brittany was nailed up in a barrel and thrown into the sea, where she gave birth to St Budoc ('the drowned one') and was miraculously fed by angels until washed up on the coast of Ireland. The Cornish saints came floating over on a variety of vessels: St Ia (patron of St Ives) upon a leaf, and a colleague upon a millstone. One Irish saint *may* even have reached North America in a boat made of leather.

But in all these navigations, the sea was an obstacle to be overcome and not a blessing like the earth. Fishing has always demanded a toll of life which farming does not exact (which may be why Christ recruited fishermen). I have searched the new Service Book in vain for the equivalent of those 1662 Forms of Prayer to be Used at Sea: but the ASB seems to have abandoned the sea as it has the weather, and the Thanksgiving after a Storm and the Prayer to be said before the Fight at Sea against any Enemy are no more – a reflection, I suppose, of Britannia's abdication of her rule over the waves. We seem to have become a landbound people who no longer do business in great waters.

I've spoken about the sea as if it were a sort of blind spot in God's vision, and I have this primitive suspicion that it may be. But seen from the land it still speaks of his mysterious ways: the way it catches and bounces the light from heaven, and above all the long, slow rhythms of the tides, cutting across our neat, efficient calendars and calling you not to do the same thing at the same time every day, but to consult and work with forces that know another law, a deeper rhythm.

Creatures Great and Small

26 September 1981

You can hardly get into Room 231 Broadcasting House these days, because of the heaps of letters requesting the companion notes for 'Priestland's Progress'. We have already sent out the entire first edition, and the second is now being stuffed into envelopes by ladies mostly called Amanda (but underneath, they're *all* lovable . . .).

I apologize if I seem to be advertising, but this is the best way to pass on some messages. The notes are in the post. They're twenty pence a copy plus stamped addressed envelope; but if you only want one or two, it's hardly economical to send a cheque. We'd rather have a postal order.

I have been reading your letters commenting on the series, and they will form the raw material for the final programme. But I'm afraid that while *you* might spend half-an-hour penning a well-wrought argument, *I* can't possibly spend several hundred half-hours replying to each personally. Among my letters, however, there is one I think I must answer at some length; both because I have had a number like it, and because it is not an issue that I'm dwelling on in the series. It concerns animals – and that (I know from experience) is a subject full of bites and scratches. Good people write to me saying that God's creatures are being exploited, tortured, neglected, they can't speak for themselves, so will I please speak for them? It is not thought well of when I respond that I'm not sure what the animals want me to say, and that on the whole I put people first.

That seems to me sound, Genesis-based theology – provided one remembers the idea of stewardship: that man was given the world of Nature not merely for his use, but to take care of – as indeed Noah did, in a splendid example to all of us. If we continue along the lines of the Old Testament, we find various rules about the care and sacrifice of animals and the consumption of animal produce. The New Testament tells us that God remembers every sparrow, but 'Ye are of more value than many sparrows'.

So it seems to me that cruelty or the cynical exploitation of animals are out – as much because of what they do to us and say about us, as because of what they do to the animals. But I think a tendency to run the world, or even one's own life, putting the animals first would be to get things upside down: *Ye* are of more value. We have to respect the animals (for they are God's creatures, even if we have called them into existence), but we must also beware of idolatry. Biblically it is we, not they, who are created in God's image; we who know God – and we who can sin.

Animals do not necessarily live worse lives today than in that mythical golden age of harmony and interdependence. It seems to me quite legitimate for us to make use of animals, even as pets. Pets run a graver risk of being worshipped as idols, but they can be psychologically good for us when they fill gaps in the exchange of love, and help love to flow.

And so I come to my letter, which came from a lady who was heart-broken over the death of her Siamese cat. Though married, with children and grandchildren, she wrote, 'I just can't reconcile myself to her loss. Is she, do you think, enjoying eternal sunshine? Or, when I laid her in the earth, was that the end?' I wrote back saying it was not, since the affection and beauty of the cat plainly lived on as part of her owner, and would surely go with her, wherever her spirit went. But not being a reincarnationist – and finding no evidence in the Christian tradition, which I trust – I could not honestly say that cats had immortal souls. I may be wrong. I don't see how the Bible can be expected to answer everything. But it does say firmly: Thou shalt love the Lord thy God, and thy neighbour and thy father and mother. Animals are on a different page.

Hold Fast

3 October 1981

I skipped lunch the other day to meet a man who has skipped every meal for the past week, and will be skipping them all for the next fortnight. In other words, he is fasting continuously for three weeks, in solidarity with the people of Northern Ireland. I find what he is doing both moving and morally impeccable. It is important to realize that it is on quite a different level from the H-block hunger-strikers, even though it does reach out to them.

In the porch of St Margaret's, Westminster – looking out over Westminster Abbey churchyard, towards the humming traffic of Victoria Street – sits a handsome young man with curly hair and a small wooden cross round his neck. His name is John Gyte, and with him sits his fragile-looking French wife, Michèle. When I was there, they had the company of a lady from Suffolk who had brought her two dogs along: an obedient half-pointer and an elderly, intractable basset. John Gyte sipped a little hot water, with salt, from a teacup: they might have been a family party who'd stopped to rest their feet. There was nothing theatrical or headline-grabbing about it.

John and Michèle belong to a community known as 'The Ark of Lanza del Vasto', perhaps better known by its French name of *L'Arche*; it's near Montpelier in France. Lanza was an Italian nobleman, a follower of the Mahatma Gandhi, and his community is based on Gandhian principles (plus a pinch of Quakerism). Its members are required to follow their own religions; it preaches no new doctrine and seeks the reconciliation of faiths. Ark members work with their hands to supply their own needs. And while they profess no politics, they work for political reconciliation through non-violence. That is what John Gyte is trying to do at St Margaret's. The church authorities lock him into the vestry every night, by the way, and reckon he's good for security.

If you go to see him, he'll give you four very carefully worded documents: the first, 'A Call to Conscience Concerning the State of Violence in Northern Ireland', and then three letters addressed to the hunger-strikers, to Mrs Thatcher, and to the British people. John has no personal involvement in Ireland, but he says that, as an Englishman, he is aware of great wrongs and violence inflicted on Ireland by the English over eight hundred years; yet at no time has Britain ever admitted or apologized for her fundamental injustice towards her neighbour. He acknowledges to Mrs Thatcher that the rights of the Unionist population must be respected; but, he says, our treatment of that population must also bear in mind Britain's responsibility for the origins and escalation of the crisis.

To the British people, John Gyte declares that peace demands pardon and that if we are prepared to look honestly at our relations with Ireland over the centuries, it is clear that we have a great moral debt to pay.

To the hunger-strikers, he writes, 'If I refuse the violent acts made in my country's name, I must equally refuse those violent acts you have used. These acts do not elevate either the Irish or the British. They bind us all in hate and recrimination. A renunciation of violence would open the hearts of many British people.' But he also tells the hunger-strikers, 'If we can but share a time of common hardship together, I will be content.'

And that is the impeccably Gandhian root of the fast. The Call to Conscience says, 'It is not undertaken as a threat, nor as an attempt to pressurize . . . It is a means of assuming on myself the anguish and pain of all the Northern Ireland people, regardless of their beliefs. It is an act of solidarity with all those who are victims of terror and violence, from whichever side. I do not claim any new peace initiative, nor do I condone the use of violence, which cannot be accepted in any cause.' John Gyte calls upon us to join him in prayer or in token fasting.

You can dismiss him for not crying 'Smash the IRA!' or 'Brits Out!' according to taste. You may think his reading of history naïve. But you cannot, I think, question his rare cleanness of purpose.

Simple Faith

10 October 1981

Letters of comment have been rolling in about 'Priestland's Progress'. I'm glad to say many of them are appreciative and constructive. To those who say they would like to ponder the programmes at a more relaxed pace, may I suggest the weekly summaries in *The Listener,* or the expanded book of the series, or the cassettes.

There have also been communications from some of the less conventional churches (most of which insist they are the one true church, as founded by the apostles): among which I shall always cherish the Church of the Seven Thunders, whose theology appears to be based on the discovery that the three frogs issuing from the mouths of the beasts in Revelation represent the heretical doctrine of the Trinity. Once you've realized that, it seems, everything looks quite different. Then there is the gentleman who has proved – to his own satisfaction – that only St John's gospel is really Christian, and the other three are virtually pagan.

Two themes, however, keep recurring among my letters, and I should like to deal with them this morning. One is, 'Why don't you just affirm the simple truths of the Bible?' and the other, 'You are undermining the Christian faith with your doubts – at worst, you are not a Christian!'

The first thing I have to say about the Bible is that we wouldn't have the Christian faith in any form without it. As Mr Roy Plomley acknowledges, there has to be one on every desert island; and to those who find its truth simple, I would say, 'God bless you – and keep right on! You certainly don't need me.' For I do not find it simple – nor do most of those I've interviewed who have spent a lifetime studying it. You may call us a bunch of fouled-up intellectuals who will never enter God's kingdom, because we arrogantly refuse to become as little children; but I think we have to take a chance on that. If God has given one an enquiring mind, I think he intends one to use it, though goodness knows life would be a lot easier without it.

To call the truth of the Bible simple is, I think, to devalue it and rob it of its richness: and it is that richness which has kept it alive and growing – for I don't see it as set solid for all time. New meanings are constantly rising to the surface, called forth by the workings of the spirit within its readers. In any case, I don't see how we can pretend that our meanings and modes of thought – let alone our way of life –

are identical with those of writers who may have lived up to four thousand years ago. We have constantly to ask ourselves, 'What must the truth be *now* if people who thought as they did wrote this?' Must we still put adulterers to death – decline to wear clothing of mixed fibres? Are we better Christians for refusing to allow women to speak in church, or to pray without a hat?

I think some of my correspondents have in mind less trivial details than that. How can I dare (they wonder) even to examine the divinity of Jesus, or the meaning of the sacrifice upon the Cross? Surely I am undermining those of weaker faith? (Never the correspondent, by the way – he or she is always doubtful of other people's abilities to think for themselves.)

I hope I'm not guilty of inverted snobbery when I say that I always work on the assumption that my listeners are at least as clever as I am and perfectly capable of seeing through my errors. And I am quite certain that the Christian faith – which has endured twenty centuries of nit-picking – will be able to shrug off mine. But in a world that seethes with intellectual speculation, some of it really subversive, I do not think Christians serve their Lord by leaving it all to the secularists.

If there is one representative listener I would like to help, it is this one, near Oxford: 'Many of us', she writes, 'find church services a complete put-off, and aggressive Christians an even greater put-off. Often one is left feeling that it is an exclusive club which we can never expect to join. Their lack of charity of thought makes one rush for the safety of agnosticism.'

On Being Prepared

17 October 1981

Last night, having spent the whole week on what has become the Priestland's Progress industry, I said to my wife, in despair, 'What am I going to do for Yours Faithfully? I haven't an idea left in my head.'

Wives live a great deal closer to reality than husbands who work at the BBC; so when, after cooking the supper and stroking the cat a bit, mine suggested, 'Why don't you talk about Preparing?', I gratefully accepted that she was on to something. How should we prepare ourselves, for life, for death, failure, success, particularly if we are religious people?

One turns immediately to the Bible, and there are those who regard it almost as a substitute for preparation. Faced with a problem, they look up some relevant passage or even open it at random and read off the answer. There must be limits to this, for it sounds dangerously close to treating God as a cosmic repair-man or puppet-master, instead of using the free will he has endowed us with. It is right to let the scriptures educate us about the nature of God generally; but absurd, surely, to imagine we will find his detailed blueprint for our daily lives in them. Constantly we are compelled to choose, to exercise our freedom, to risk sinning, to live spontaneously and adventurously. One thing the Bible does tell us is that we are bound to sin and should not be afraid of that; because if, like the prodigal son, we make a mess of things, we have only to return penitently to the Father and we shall be forgiven. We should never be afraid of failure. For ultimately the universe is on our side, and we shall be prepared for almost anything if we trust in that.

Jesus himself was a very interesting mixture of preparedness and unpreparedness. He does not seem to have studied religion systematically, but he was a self-made preacher and prophet, and we know he spent some time in the wilderness before embarking upon his ministry. He prepared his disciples for their ministry: but what really counted with them was the dynamic charge they received from the experience of his resurrection and Holy Spirit. No amount of hint-dropping by their Lord could prepare them for what happened between the Last Supper and Pentecost. As they journeyed through Palestine with him, they were told to take no heed for the morrow, what they should eat or wear, and though the advice appropriate to wandering holy men is not necessarily right for a working man with a family to care for, almost all religions do warn us against getting obsessed with material things. I do not think Christianity is against our enjoying them, but it points firmly away from making them the object of life.

One reason is that they are the slaves of time and we must not be, because our worth is eternal.

Preparation and time are perilously bound up together. Was it W.B. Yeats who cried, desolately, 'The whole of my life has been a preparation for something that never happened'? Where he went wrong was in thinking it was not happening all the time. Even to think of life as a preparation for death is wrong, if we imagine that our death must be some time in the distant future. For any of us, it could be *now*. One can learn a great deal from a short stay in an Intensive Care Unit.

So the important thing is not preparing but being prepared. For what? Christians would say for judgement. And that means for reconciliation with God. Since God dwells deep within us, we must learn to live deep, where we can come to terms with ourselves. If the divine in us and the human in us are reconciled, then we are prepared for anything, including the most abject failure. Fame, money, superficial success are not what ultimately matter.

As for helping to prepare others, like our children, it is a mistake to try to nail down the future for them too firmly. The most important thing is our own example of what we are now, and the help we give our children to become what they truly are (though Heaven knows it can be hard enough finding that out). We worry too much. We trust too little. Most of us need to calm down and stop thinking we must have all the answers in advance.

No Way Out

24 October 1981

I have had a number of letters recently that make me weep with a mixture of rage and sorrow. For they come from people who have suffered for years from the cruel parody they have conceived of the Christian faith: not as a message of forgiveness and life, but as a code of punishment and death. I shall do my best to answer those letters personally, and I certainly shall not identify their writers here; but I would like to share some of them with you this morning. Heavens knows, I am not qualified in pastoral care – would that my correspondents had turned somewhere else – but doing this may just stop one or two people driving over the edge. It will also let off a bit of my steam.

Here's an elderly gentleman whose dear wife died after more than forty years of marriage. 'Suppose I can't go on without you?' he asked her on her deathbed. 'Would it be all right if I took a short cut?' 'Yes,' she said, 'because my God is compassionate, and would understand, and we would be together again.' So he has joined a certain organization, which has given him its literature on the subject, and he wonders if he ought to take that short cut now, before he has the option removed from him by some paralysing complaint. Please don't, my friend. God is indeed compassionate. I would not criticize your dear wife for thinking of herself, as she did. She will see things differently now. How do you know what plans *God* may have for you? Even, perhaps, the chance to draw out the love and service of someone who will nurse you one day. Don't force God's hand. His will be done – not yours – not even your dear wife's.

But that did not make me angry, only sad. Here's a letter from a lady brought up in a fine Christian home, with no real worries, blessed in many ways (she says) and yet devastated by waves of despair. 'People think I live a blameless life, trying to do good,' she writes, 'but I feel I'm walking a tightrope, and if I don't keep to the high standards of my denomination, I shall fall off. This is not Life Abundant. My religion is more of a worry than a blessing, so there is something wrong with it. I look around at the carefree, jolly people who enjoy life and are not apparently troubled in any way by their lack of Christianity. And yet the true Christians seem to have a peace which I lack.'

It is clear enough to me that, first, that lady's church has failed utterly to convince her of the Gospel of love and forgiveness; and, second, she might very well benefit from talking out her feelings of guilt with a psychiatrist.

I heard another lady who 'talked it out' by writing a long, unpublished book about it. At the age of thirteen, she came upon that passage in St Mark about the unforgivable sin against the Holy Ghost. 'That was the end of life for me', she writes. 'The sun vanished and I was sick with fear and afraid to speak to anybody for fear of being laughed at. The next twenty years were sheer hell, because I was afraid I had committed this sin.'

I have met several cases like that. The failure of people to find explanations of that mysterious sin has caused untold suffering. There are similar texts in Matthew and Luke, and from their settings, I think there are two possible explanations: either Christ is urging Christians not to crack under persecution, or he is denouncing those who allege that he casts out evil spirits by the power of the Devil. I do not think many of my listeners will even have the opportunity of committing those sins. Indeed, I venture to suggest that most of our sins are too boring and banal to get us within miles of hell fire. We need to stop wailing, to repent, take our forgiveness, and get back to the business of loving one another.

Jack Dominian, the Christian psychiatrist, once told me: 'Christianity has failed abysmally to help people see that when they feel guilty, they do not have to reject themselves as totally bad. Both Protestant and Catholic traditions have given us a wholly unChristian view of Man over this. Nowhere in the Bible is there a sense that sin separates man completely from God. You never lose the love of God.'

Whom God Hath Joined

31 October 1981

Marriage and divorce are my subject this morning – prompted by the appearance of two books (or rather, one book and a pamphlet) by people who command my particular respect and affection: Dr Jack Dominian,* Roman

Catholic psychiatrist; and Monica Furlong,** with whom I once shared an office where no work got done at all because we spent the whole time helpless with laughter – and it's typical of so many-sided a person that at that very time she was going through the agony of her divorce, about which she has written in this pamphlet. That illustrates one personal conviction of my own: that moralizers about divorce should be very careful indeed of deploring the lightness with which people dissolve their marriages. From my observations it is seldom a light matter: it certainly wasn't in Mrs Furlong's case. 'I was a Christian,' she writes, 'and *we* didn't go in for divorce. We made our bed, and by God, we lay on it.' Eventually, after some twenty years, she could no longer pretend she was living in a marriage at all.

'What I am coming to see', she continues, 'is not that Christians have a "high" doctrine of marriage, but that on the contrary, they have a pitifully low one, often encouraging people to get married who should never do so, and feeling sorry for those who do not choose to get married off. Marriage does not automatically solve any human problems. The slogan ought to be "Fewer and Better".' Mrs Furlong thinks that Christian intransigence towards divorce stems from the fear that it may be poor propaganda for the Church. But where is the Gospel of forgiveness in thinking it so dreadful to have made a mistake? She concludes, 'Christianity is on the side of life, not of living death.'

Monica Furlong's booklet *Divorce* is published broadmindedly by the Mothers' Union – with a note that 'the views of the author are her own, and do not necessarily reflect those of the membership'.

There is just as much compassion and understanding built into Jack Dominian's book *Marriage, Faith & Love.* But I should warn you that it is rather clinically written for the doctor, priest and counsellor rather than for the literary voyeur. And it is written from the Roman Catholic point of view. But in fact, centuries of what I must call in the best sense 'casuistry' (that is, the application of ethical rules to special cases) have produced a far more commonsense and flexible approach than some of the high-mindedness on the Protestant side.

Dr Dominian is no Vatican hack, in any case. He explains very clearly why marriage is a Christian sacrament (actually, it took the Church itself a long time to make up its mind about this), but he points to many of the same conclusions as Monica Furlong about marriages which are not really marriages at all, marriages (as he puts it) which are so only in name because the psychological resources of loving are not present. They are, in Catholic terms, null. Some people, I suppose, will find the development of nullity in this way an example of Catholic dodginess – of achieving divorce by another name; but there is a great deal of psychological truth behind it.

There is certainly nothing dodgy about Dr Dominian's attitude towards premarital sex and living together. People, he says, are scared of committing themselves, and one should always ask why. The fact remains that marriage has a public as well as a private dimension; society needs clarity in human relationships, and to forfeit this not only confuses and threatens society, it denies the couple any support they might claim as a result of being married. Personally, I'd like to ask society what (if anything) it thinks it is doing to help marriage these days. But I agree with Dr Dominian that sex is not the best way of finding out if two people are suited to each other. Availability, Reliability, Continuity – these are the things he stresses.

* *Marriage, Faith & Love,* by Jack Dominian, Darton, Longman & Todd, £7.50.

** *Divorce,* by Monica Furlong, Mothers' Union, 80p.

Racism and Faith

7 November 1981

Members of the forthcoming General Synod of the Church of England have, as usual, a lot of paper to get through; but I hope they will give special attention to a slim yellow booklet and a fat white book.

The yellow one will certainly produce some yells: *The Church of England and Racism*, it's called, and it's the report of a Consultation of some fifty people, held in a Leicester monastery early last month. Among those attending were the Bishop of London, representatives of such bodies as 'Christians against Racism and Fascism', and clergy from Liverpool, Manchester and Southall.

The language is of a kind to produce knee-jerk reactions, though whether you jerk with rage or enthusiasm may be connected with whether you read the *Guardian* or the *Telegraph*. How do you react to such statements as 'Racism has become institutionalized in the Church of England'? Does it actually tell you anything at all, even when it goes on to speak of 'the still-prevailing Anglican ideology which sees itself as white, right and essentially changeless'?

Part of the trouble with this booklet is that its authors have gone galloping ahead – crying out for more black clergy, Muslim teachers in church schools, money for the World Council's anti-Racism programme – before most of the rank-and-file infantry are convinced they want to fight that war. Shame on the infantry, you may say; how can they *not* see that this is a multi-racial, multi-cultural society which must have liberty and justice for all? It's one thing to see that in principle, another to feel it in one's guts, another again to see where the individual fits in. What one would really welcome would be literature that got through on those last two levels, instead of (for example) bashing the media for, I quote: 'Failing to report the engagement of church leaders in contentious areas of public policy.' Maybe the Church does not impress the media. In which case, this report proposes some action that might. Though not, please, uttering more handouts from Church House, as it suggests.

I suppose that other report, *Believing in The Church,* is a typical example of 'white Anglican ideology'. It is the first fruit of the current Church of England Doctrine Commission – successor to the old one, whose report *Christian Believing in The Church** is not an attempt to define *what* the Church believes, but rather *how* it believes; and I think it is well worth reading. Among individual contributions I would pick out Professor John Bowker's rather tough, scientific chapter about the nature of religious systems; and William Vanstone's piece about the Christian *story.* The importance of the 'story' to Christian belief runs right through the book; and it makes the point that stories are every bit as important as doctrine; indeed, that they carry doctrine most powerfully and need to be retold, imaginatively, in each successive generation.

Another valuable idea is this: We have gone too far in treating belief as something that is purely individual and private. In a universe of private opinions, all belief becomes relative. Nowadays we contrast it not with unbelief, but with knowledge. Yet this is nonsense. Believing is a much more corporate activity than we tend to recognize. Believing (says the report) is mainly belonging. Science, ethics, politics, the arts all depend upon membership of a certain community, upon operating within a certain consensus and being in dialogue with it – a critical dialogue, maybe, but not just talking to oneself. The report points out, astutely, that 'those who do their thinking in isolation become strangely uniform and unoriginal'.

'Tradition itself', it goes on, 'is an unceasing argument between conservation and development. Dissenters remain with the dialogue, knowing that the roots which nourish their protest run into the soil of communal belief.' Very well said.

* SPCK, £8.50.

Take It Easy

14 November 1981

I met a serene and happy person the other day – such people do exist – who said to me: 'You know, I've had an excellent life. I've got no frustrated longings. I want to go on doing what I'm doing now – hopefully a little better – but I don't terribly care what other people think of it – I'm not worried about success . . .'

Needless to say, that was a woman; and nobody could call her smug or selfish, because she devotes a great deal of her time to keeping an eye on her grown-up children and working for the elderly. By some miracle of chemistry, she just is the sort of person who instinctively follows the Christian principle that what really matters is not doing but being. This involves a certain wholeness, a certain harmony. If you can live harmoniously, you will almost certainly do harmonious things – though they may not make you famous.

A few days before that, I met a doctor who thinks the plague of our day is Overwork. 'It's incredible', he said. 'I get relays of successful men at the top of their profession – who could well afford to relax at last – and they're all running scared. When I tell a senior civil servant he's killing himself, he says he's expected to, and there's some sort of posthumous decoration for it. It's considered the honourable thing to drop dead the day you retire. But nothing's worth that.'

There is surely something crazy about the fact that while part of the population (usually the least privileged) is out of work, an approximately equal number of the most privileged is working harder than it can bear. It gets pretty well rewarded for this; but instead of enjoying those rewards, it just works harder and harder. This is partly the fault of the boss-class (which probably works harder than anyone, and illustrates survival of the fittest), but part of the blame must also rest with the workaholics themselves. They have become addicted to overwork. They would not know what to do with themselves if they stopped – though stopped they are, eventually, by one kind of disaster or another.

It is just understandable that the ambitious young, with reputations to establish, should behave like this: but it is nonsense for somebody in his forties to sixties to compete for the Nobel Prize in Self-Destruction. One of the great things about the late President Eisenhower – mocked in his day, but now wistfully respected – is that he kept taking time off from the White House to go and play golf. Would that there were more politicians on golf-courses: they do less harm there, and it gives them a chance to get dis-obsessed. Yet the proudest boast of many politicians – and businessmen, broadcasters, lawyers, you-name-them – is that they are fuller than full-time. But who are they doing it for? It's sinfully untrue that any of us is indispensable; and loving one's neighbour surely ought to begin with caring about one's wife and family – most of whom would far rather have a living husband and father than one who's dying for success.

Somebody might accuse me of undermining the national economy. For am I not calling on people to work less hard? Yes, I am. And it is not just in support of some leftwing scheme to share jobs: I dare to say it's for spiritual welfare. It's to spare people's lives, save their marriages, care for their children and cultivate what's left of their souls.

Beyond a certain point, sheer busy-ness is the enemy of religion. Hence, remember the Sabbath, to keep it holy. You cannot even pray decently without stillness – which makes me think that pop music is probably the work of the Devil. One thing that strikes me about the mission of Jesus is its leisureliness: he and his disciples simply downed tools and pottered about talking. I know there were labourers working in vineyards and grumbling about their pay, but they were not chained to production lines or, worse still, to some promotion ladder or ratings race. There are, I know, holes to be shot in what I've been saying – and perhaps exaggerating – but I think it is almost as wrong to drive one's body into an early grave as to commit suicide.

Not So Easy

21 November 1981

Last week, in an idle moment, I held forth on the evils of overwork, and berated those whose idea of a creative life seemed to be competing for the Nobel Prize in Self-Destruction. Letters have been dropping around me like autumn leaves ever since. All over Britain, it seems, wives were nudging husbands out of their Saturday lie-in, hissing

'He's talking about you!' Quite a number wrote in for copies of the script to be framed and hung up in offices – though knowing the average workaholic, they will probably end up in that bottom right-hand drawer where he keeps those forgotten travel brochures about long weekends in Paris and the book on blood-pressure. There were letters about frenetic estate agents, private investigators and bankers; but never assume this plague is confined to the city. There were quite as many West Country farmers and rural clergymen. So much for the long, slow, natural rhythms of the countryside.

One thing you learn in my position: when it comes to human behaviour, there's no rule without an exception. And the exception in this case was presented to me, most elegantly, by a correspondent whom I shall call Mr Keyes, of Cornwall.

'The cause of this disease', he writes, 'is not of the individual's own making, any more than the common cold is. It is wrong to think that most people work themselves to a standstill because they enjoy doing so. It is the fear of losing one's job and the power that often goes with it. What is more, it is not the amount of work they actually do that counts, it is what they *appear* to be doing. A person may be doing his job well and without fuss, but unless he can be seen by his employer to be working "to the limit" (so to speak), he will be for the chop. None of us is essential; but – by golly! – it pays to be thought so.'

Mr Keyes then writes from his own experience. At one time he was appointed general manager of a company that was a complete shambles. For six months he worked hard to bring order out of chaos, succeeded, and with everything running efficiently was able to ease up and do what a general manager should do. The trouble was, after two or three years, the directors reckoned they could operate just as well without him and gave him the sack. 'The mistake I had made', says Mr Keyes, 'was that I was not seen to be doing as much work as I had been. I was no longer working myself into the grave. There is a saying "Justice must not only be done – it must be seen to be done". I assure you, Mr Priestland, the same is true of work: a job must not only be done, it must be seen to be done – to the limit.' And Mr Keyes concludes that although he's quite happy now and has no regrets, he would welcome my suggestions as to the cause and cure for this malady.

The truth is, I haven't really got either: like every moralist, I denounce sin, advocate repentance and then change the subject. A few more denunciations might sound good: the ruthlessness of capitalism, the material greed of the directors, profits put before people – but Mr Keyes's enquiry remains unanswered, and I am quite sure it is not going to be answered by legislation: not with recession putting every job at risk and the ingenious Japanese purloining our very underwear. Who dares to work *less* hard in times like these? Stand by for the age of ruthlessness – it has already arrived.

And yet I see a certain hope. I really got into this subject on religious grounds, because I think overwork is the enemy not only of our own bodies and the welfare of our families, but the enemy of that occasional stillness without which there is no religious life at all and the soul starves. I do not know the condition of Mr Keyes's soul – he did not mention it – but I get the impression of a man who has learnt to rise above success and failure and, in his sixties, is now at peace with himself. One way or another, he has learnt also to forgive himself: as we are indeed forgiven.

Progressive's Progress

28 November 1981

My radio series, 'Priestland's Progress', is now in its final stages. The whole operation has yielded more letters than we can possibly respond to; but all have been read, and I'm profoundly grateful for the care people have taken with them. They have given me ideas that will nourish me for years to come.

Among them was a remarkable commentary on the series from an Anglican woman of confessed liberal tendencies, from whom I shall quote at some length; not because I want to plug her line (I do not always agree with her, by any means), but because she is stimulating – and that is really what 'Priestland's Progress' was trying to do.

Mrs D. (let us call her) does not like my patronizing the spirituality of women, for a start: 'I have found anyone who is left alone with his mind free to roam, in quiet places or up against the elements, who has spells of silence or comes up against suffering, to have an awareness of God', she says. But what God? Mrs D. firmly rejects SUPERCHAP – 'the personal yet perfect God. Like Spike Milligan, I feel that if God were a chap, he would be imperfect. But then I believe that there is "that of God in everyone"' (she writes), 'God is not a medicine injected into me. God is programmed into every cell. That is the only sense I can make of talking about God.'

Mrs D. will not have anything to do with the notion of death as evil, the punishment for sin. 'Look at Genesis. The reaction to Adam and Eve acquiring technology (the Knowledge of Good and Evil – nothing to do with morals, but with science): God's reaction is "Quick, get them out of Eden before they eat from the Tree of Life and acquire immortality!"'

But Mrs D. is much preoccupied with sin, or perhaps with the Church's preoccupation. She wishes it would not keep saying, '"Lord have mercy on us!" like some wretched child screaming at an angry parent – "Daddy, don't hit me!" The word *mercy* was a mistranslation where the Hebrew conveyed the meaning of *steadfast love*. All the whimpering and sobbing and sighing for mercy should never have happened.' Mrs D. goes on, 'Get the whole thing privatized into me and Superchap, and you begin to feel trapped. St Paul, whatever he said, could not overcome his feeling that everything costs something. God's forgiveness could not be free, so he found his explanation of the Cross as a sacrifice for sin very liberating. And I don't believe that God is just. Justice is what my enemy *ought* to grant – a measly minimum. It always operates *un*justly, too. Love is never content to be just; its measure always runs over. There is no bargaining in love, so the Cross was not a bargain. Forgiveness, and the whole Jesus system, says "Here we are. What is the way to create the most possible good out of this mess?" It never says, "Whodunnit? Who's to blame?" The cause of suffering, on the Jesus system, is far less important than how it can best be used to the glory of God. It can be an earthing of evil through the sufferer. Pain, loss, tribulation HAS to happen. Without it there could be no change, no happenings, no joy. Light without shade has no meaning. Total bliss is oblivion.'

To Mrs D. the Cross exposes the utter irrelevance of power or success. She writes, 'If Superchap were arranging things deliberately from a position of total knowledge and power, that would be very depressing news. But if God is continuously being defeated by the crassness of things, then I'm more than ready to accept the idea of working to foster his chances.'

Mrs D. is a sister depressive (as you might have guessed): 'I can't quite see how God, though He *is* love, can be said to love me', she says wistfully. '*You* keep mentioning your experience of a loving God. It would be nice to experience being loved. However, I don't ever recall feeling wicked. My evangelical friends tell me this is why I cannot get the joyous experience of being a born-again Christian.'

Pop Goes the Devil

5 December 1981

Reverberations continue from the piece I did a few weeks ago about the mortal sin of overwork – one or two Puritan listeners sternly insisting that, on the contrary, work was ordained as a punishment from God and there is no scriptural authority for the five-day week. Six days shalt thou labour . . . and what's more, thou hadst better be up by five a.m.

In the course of my dissertation, I remarked that busyness was the enemy of religion, and that one could not even pray decently without stillness: which made me think that pop music was probably the work of the Devil. Cue for more protests, though from a rather different constituency. These talks are not exactly top of the pops with teenagers, but some of those who were listening found that remark the last straw – the generation gap excavated into the pit of Hell. One listener wrote enthusiastically of how Africans drummed and danced their acts of worship – so why shouldn't Europeans?

Well, for a start, I wasn't talking about the sort of liturgical dancing or folk masses one occasionally meets – let alone *Godspell* and *Jesus Christ Superstar*. One can argue about whether it helps or hinders the religious message to set it to rhythms that summon up the sexy throb of a discotheque. Still, great composers have mixed religious words and secular music before now. What I am talking about is the hypnotic, spirit-deadening effect of nonstop pop (in which I lump, indiscriminately, Reggae, Rock, Disco and all kinds of electronic bumping and grinding). I had better be careful here to distinguish between my own middle-aged prejudice and what I believe to be an objective danger. I really detest ninety per cent of modern pop, which seems to me monotonous and crude beyond words – reducing the heavenly vocabulary of music to a scream and a thump. But, okay, you keep the Heavy Metal out of my hair and I'll keep Sibelius out of yours. One also has to recognize, I think, that their purposes are rather different. The main purpose of a classical symphony is to explore various forms and relationships, to resolve various conflicts. That of pop music nowadays is to excite – more or less actively – the sense of dance: and that's fine, especially if you are dancing. Except that, if left on all the time, it drowns anything else and renders us incapable of receiving any other messages from the universe around us, or of thinking what they mean. In short, it anaesthetizes the religious ear; and if I were the Devil, I would think it a major triumph to have piped pop music in every supermarket and pub, a music-centre in every bedsit, a transistor in every workshop. 'We've got to stamp out anything approaching contemplation' (says the Devil), 'or that creep the Holy Spirit will wriggle into the silence. Turn up the sound level!'

Actually, unlike some of my listeners, I don't believe in a personal Devil. I think it's really us: us being lazy and frightened – frightened of being alone in the depths, where God is; Light surrounded by Darkness, Silence surrounded by Uproar.

But, oh dear! I am sounding pious and priggish. In fact I am not at all sure that I really *want* the pop-lovers (who are mostly young) to switch off their cassette-players and tune in full time to God. I shall now give enormous offence by saying that nothing alarms me more – not even a pile of Reggae records – than a certain kind of piety in the young. No doubt it shows up my own failings, but when I meet someone who is sure of his faith before he is sixty, I wonder, 'Where is he going to *grow*?' I admire faith like old shoes: full of holes and not too shiny – faith that has been somewhere and taken a few wrong turnings – not a faith that's never put a foot wrong. I sometimes think the Hindus have the right idea in not expecting much religion of the young: that comes later in life, when the shoes are worn.

In the meantime – to make a sharp U-turn – perhaps we should be grateful for pop music in these unemployed times. Karl Marx could hardly maintain that religion was the opiate of the people. Today, surely, it's pop music.

To Covenant with Whom?

12 December 1981

1981 will go down in ecclesiastical history as the year in which the major non-Roman churches in England all but agreed to move on towards unity by covenant. As the year draws to a close, voices are being raised urging that 1982 should become the year in which they drew back. Most recently, two distinguished Anglican bishops – John Moorman and Edward Knapp-Fisher – have written to *The Times* urging that the first priority of the Church of England should be communion with Rome, and that Anglicans should at least postpone entering into covenant with other churches. It is reasonable to suppose that the two bishops were conscious of the forthcoming visit to Great Britain by the Pope.

Nor are Anglican Catholics the only party to be having second thoughts – or rather, boosting their first ones. A key issue in the Covenant for nonconformists is the proposal to accept the historic episcopacy by converting their moderators into bishops; and this has brought some powerful opposition among the United Reformed, including such names as Vernon Sproxton, Geoffrey Nuttall and Daniel Jenkins. Briefly, they deny that the succession from the apostles can be proved, or that there were bishops (as such) in apostolic times; and they see the proposal to adopt them as a capitulation to Anglican arrogance and author itarianism with nothing yielded in exchange. 'We may well find', says Dr Jenkins, 'that we have appointed captains to lead us back to Egypt, only to discover that Pharaoh doesn't want us.'

Another group of Free Church ministers and laity nailed their theses symbolically to the door of Canterbury Cathedral: 'Freechurchmanship', they declared, 'cannot accept such forms. It derives from the practice of the apostolic church of the New Testament, which had neither priests nor a hierarchical structure based on episcopal concepts.'

There is support for this in a pro-Covenant Catholic booklet, just published by the SPCK, arguing that for two hundred years bishops were chosen by their communities and did not necessarily receive any laying-on of hands. The booklet opposes what it calls 'the Catholic Tridentine view' that a priest has private and indelible powers to celebrate the Mass, quite distinct from his relation to the community.

All of which goes to show how wide a gap still exists between different views of ministry, whatever progress may have been made in the abstract by the Anglican/

Roman Catholic International Commission, to which Bishops Moorman and Knapp-Fisher belonged. Their letter brought a response from Canon Trevor Beeson of Westminster Abbey, in which he listed five points on which Rome would have to give way before many Anglicans could take seriously the restoration of communion.

'There must be freedom', he said, 'for (1) the laity to play their full part, (2) the clergy to marry, (3) women to be ordained, (4) theologians to publish and teach freely, and (5) individuals to make their own decisions on such matters as contraception.' Canon Beeson's letter was flanked by one from Professor James Atkinson (an authority on Luther) denying the assumption that Protestants had *left* the Church and must *return* to the fold, and demanding: 'When the Holy Father comes to these shores, will someone tell him that Protestantism is not, and never was, lapsed Catholicism, but the most creative and significant interpretation of Christianity since apostolic times?'

Now it seems to me that the most generous ecumenical gesture that the Pope could make would be to go some way towards acknowledging Professor Atkinson's claims. It is just conceivable. But what is inconceivable is that he would accept Canon Beeson's, and it is my guess that in choosing ecumenical partners the average churchgoer is more impressed by what other churches actually do than by how they define the Eucharist or the episcopacy. There's a good deal of talking together between Roman Catholics and members of other churches; but from what I hear, very little doing.

The Tragedy of Life

19 December 1981

Overheard the other day at a party: 'Life is such a tragedy . . .'

The tragedy was that anyone should say such a thing: for I don't believe it is tragic. By which, I suppose, I mean that my life is not tragic, and I do not have a tragic view of other people's. But if I think for a moment, I can remember the days when I used to, and it must be the same for others.

It all seemed so pointless: one was born, with luck spent a few years romping in the nursery with the Christmas presents, and then slog, slog, slog, all the way to the cemetery, very occasionally sharing a moment's pleasure with some other member of the rat-race. Then they died, too. It hardly seemed worth it. One only lived for fear of dying.

And if, indeed, life were like that, it would be a tragedy. It seems to me that that kind of life would have only two things to commend it: getting as much pleasure out of it as you possibly could, or blindly obeying the call of your genes to perpetuate the species. But neither of these turns out to be very satisfying as an objective. Pleasure, besides being highly perishable, is at its best as a by-product of something else: but what? If you have no higher purpose in life, it's hard to say. There are limits to the amount of breeding one cares to do: and that, too, raises questions about the purposes. Love – in a less carnal sense – becomes important; but if that, as well, does not have a guiding purpose it can lead to other tragedies: the tragedy of being unloved, unlovable, deprived of the loved one. What's the good of loving someone if death is liable to snatch them away?

Once I watched a young girl nurse a pet kitten through death. It had been hit by a car and was dribbling blood. 'Don't die, Dee-dee,' she whispered, 'don't die. I'll do anything if you won't die.' Gradually, the glossy neck drooped, the black eyes stared without seeing. 'Dee-dee, where have you gone?' cried the girl. And wept. Then, with the ancient wisdom of her sex, she wrapped the tiny body ritually in a blanket and laid it very slowly in its box. All I could do was to touch her, and tell her that people who never loved never suffered – that love held joy in one hand, pain in the other: you had to have both. I might have said (though it did not seem appropriate for a kitten) that you could not have resurrection without death. Was the crucifixion tragic? Only if you do not know about Easter. Anyway, there's a new kitten now – and a girl who has learnt something she had to face some day.

So life's sad at times, but it is not a tragedy. If it were that, it would be absurd; and as a wise priest once said to me: 'We give ourselves away all the time – even atheists – we do not act as if life were absurd.' And surely one cannot whistle in the dark continuously for three score years and ten. Most of us sense, I think, that we have a purpose, even if we are not quite sure what it is. Seeing it is God's purpose, having to do with some further existence, it is unlikely that we should be sure. I think it involves developing our faculties of love, which we shall need wherever we're going – hence that tenderness for the dying kitten was far from wasted. To be unable to love is close to being in Hell.

But cheer up! For the Christian message, blared in our ears like a carol at Christmas time, is that God loves *us*, whether we like it or not. And that, in a rather different way, *is* absurd: it just does not fit – Almighty God, Lord of the Universe, sending himself as a helpless, messy baby into an insanitary stable in the Middle East? Gods don't behave like that! And yet, says the story, he did – out of sheer love. The only way we can resolve the conflict is to explode with laughter. Once again, life's just beginning. Call that a tragedy? Ridiculous.

On the Feast of Stephen

26 December 1981

Good morning, and a merry Feast of Stephen to you – for that's what it is. If you should happen to look out and see a poor man, your duty goes without saying. It was an ancient custom, after Christmas, to feed up the poor in the hope they would survive the harsh months that lay ahead.

But why is it also called Boxing Day? Some say the origin lies in the fact that the original Stephen was appointed by the apostles to distribute alms to the needy, especially widows. The boxes came later: they were the collecting boxes rattled under the noses of wealthy citizens by crossing sweepers, horse-holders and link-men, who made walking through London on an eighteenth-century Boxing Day quite an ordeal. Ninety years ago, in Derbyshire, my father remembered the Christmas mummers, whose chorus was 'I've got a little box under my arm, Some of your coppers would do it no harm. I've got a little box made of wood: Some of your silver would do it some good.' There followed a battle between St George and a Turk . . .

The Feast of Stephen – like that of his Lord and Saviour – got commercialized, of course. But Stephen, as the first martyr of the Christian Church, occupies a very considerable position. According to the Book of Acts, he was one of those Jews who had been abroad and spoke Greek (rather than Aramaic) as his principal language. When the Greek-speaking Christians began to complain that they were being discriminated against, Stephen was the first of seven deacons to be ordained – by laying-on of hands – to look after them. He is described as 'full of faith – full of God's grace and power, who did great wonders and miraculous signs among the people'. Stephen, then, is not only the first to be ordained in that under-estimated order of deacons – he is the first outsider to be set apart in ministry. But he evidently went beyond mere welfare work.

The Acts of the Apostles tells his story. Stephen assumed a mission to those Greek-speaking Jews who had been prisoners of Rome and then returned to Jerusalem. He shocked them with the Christian message, and they reported him to the Sanhedrin for preaching the destruction of the Temple and the replacement of the Law of Moses.

At his trial, Stephen is depicted as offering a re volutionary view of Jewish history: that far from following Moses devotedly, Israel had rejected his leadership. Instead of keeping to the simple faith of the wilderness, they had erected a nearly idolatrous Temple, with all its futile rituals. Compared with the earlier teachings of Peter, Stephen's message was a kind of Protestantism.

It could hardly have been expected to do him much good. Instead of defending himself, Stephen attacks, and culminates his speech with a vision of the heavens opening and the Son of Man standing at the right hand of God. He is dragged out of the city and stoned to death – his murderers laying their cloaks at the feet of a young man called Saul, the future St Paul. 'Lord Jesus, receive my spirit', prays the martyr; and then, echoing his Master, 'Do not hold this sin against them.' When he had said this, he fell asleep.

Violent persecution of the Christians followed. But the

implication of Acts is that it fell less upon the original Palestinian apostles than upon the new Hellenized Christians whom Stephen represented. The Greek-speakers were scattered, and the faith began to spread.

Stephen's tomb was discovered in the year 415, and his bones removed first to Byzantium and then to Rome, with the usual dispersal of bits and pieces. There was also a profitable market in genuine stones, guaranteed to have been used at his martyrdom. He became one of the most popular mediaeval saints (forty-six ancient churches being dedicated to him in England alone): the patron saint of deacons and efficacious in the treatment of headaches. One wonders, irreverently, whether Stephen could have anything to do with the bad old custom of 'getting stoned'? Anyway, it's his feast today – unless you're an Eastern Christian, in which case it's tomorrow.

Ring in the New

2 January 1982

Happy New Year to you! Doesn't life feel different – or doesn't it? In fact, New Years are an arbitrary sort of thing: they could begin at almost any time; and if you're a Jew, a Muslim or a Buddhist, that time is not now.

Our year begins in the depths of winter, which is odd. There's no sense of the cycle of life beginning all over again, though I seem to remember some lines by one of the Latin poets (perhaps Ovid) to the effect that, under the ground the seeds are germinating and the bulbs starting to push their way up. I hope they will take their time: for though I look forward to spring, I am unhappy about flowers out of season, and I like to see the trees leafless, making significant gestures against the sky. I like, too, to see the land asleep for a while; not constantly goaded into producing crops.

It's an extension, perhaps, of the hankering for silence – for a season of contemplation after months of business. One cannot always be putting out: there must be a period of taking in, as well. So it is a time to stay indoors, to read and listen and talk and think. All of which presupposes a home to do it in: not just a building to keep out the cold (though too many people have not even got that), but a familiar routine among people and things you can rely on. Reliability, surely, is the great neglected virtue. The rare flash of brilliance is nice while it lasts; but what one really needs in life is the confidence that everyday things will be there when wanted and will not break down – this applies to husbands, wives and children as well as motorcars. It is also one of the characteristics of God: never mind the miracles, feel the everlasting love – but I'm getting religious.

1982 (I can confidently predict) will not be very different from 1981. Perhaps slightly better, if only because even-number years simply look more comfortable than odd numbers. And if you look up the one-thousand-nine-hundred-and-eighty-second verse of the Bible – which, by my calculations comes as early as Exodus chapter 16 – you will find it refers to Aaron setting a pot of manna before the Ark of the Covenant. Manna being a gift of God's bounty, could it be that this refers to North Sea oil? Or that somebody will leave a fortune to the Church – but if so, which church? Study the papers minutely enough and you are sure to find something that fulfils the prophecy: though the great thing about prophecies is that everyone forgets them in a day or two.

So I can predict with even greater confidence that 1982

will be Royal Baby year, and that the child will be a girl if it is not a boy. A noted religious leader will visit Great Britain about the end of May, and there will be protests outside Canterbury Cathedral. There will be a scandal over claims that Jesus did not really die upon the Cross, and still more books about the Holy Shroud of Turin. There will be more defections to the Social Democrats, and several leading trade unionists will declare that they have never seen such derisory pay offers, nor found their members more bitter and frustrated. Both the Derby and the Grand National will be won by four-legged horses.

All of which is no more than intelligent – and in some cases informed – anticipation. But there's no promise it will really turn out that way: not because God is capricious and unreliable, but because he leaves us a hair-raising amount of free will to make our own choices. From time to time I hear from people who seek to demonstrate there is no God, on the grounds that if there were he would dash around stopping things from going wrong. If he did, life really would be predictable and, consequently, extremely boring. Not only would nobody ever die in floods or earthquakes, but nobody would die of anything at all; for, deprived of suffering (and he'd fix that, surely), we would all have good reasons for not wanting to die just yet. Life would have no shape, nothing unexpected, nothing to bite on. If God had meant us to know what was going to happen in 1982, it would be 1983 already.

Living Together

9 January 1982

This is the first chance I've had to thank those listeners who generously – if misguidedly – voted me 'Runner-up of the Year' in the 'Today' programme. I was firmly put in my place by a Scottish neighbour who observed drily that she was brought up to come first or nowhere. Actually, I don't approve of media-people being taken so seriously – one good parish priest caring for his flock is worth a dozen people like me – but I should like to think it is religion in general that is being taken seriously, far more seriously than most editors realize. If I'm learning anything from the letters that are still swamping my office, it is that 'out there', where you are, there are thousands upon thousands of unorthodox believers relieved to hear somebody expressing, in public, the doubts and convictions they have all been ashamed to confess. For it seems to me that the Christian faith, at any rate, is not a set of unreasonable certainties – it is a collection of reasonable uncertainties; and when I say 'reasonable' I do not mean the same as 'logical'. You cannot work it out like a chemical formula. But you do not – I maintain – have to treat it like a magic spell, either. So, with all respect to the churches (which we need for several good reasons), let us get religion out from under the Gothic arches and into the pubs and parties and family lunches. As for keeping Religion out of Politics – I think it might refresh that weary old war-horse enormously.

It might also, by the look of things, refresh the battered institution of marriage. As if you didn't know it, more and more couples these days are simply living together without the blessings of clergy or registrar, and a very interesting study of the phenomenon, called *Living Together*,* has been written by Clare Dyer and Marcel Berlins.

After all, says your modern secular couple, why get married? The social stigma of cohabiting has largely vanished – even illegitimacy need not handicap a child any more. There are tax advantages in cohabiting; fewer and fewer *dis*advantages, and I've even heard it argued that if you do not get married, you will never become a divorce statistic (though there is some pretty trivial thinking involved there).

Subconsciously, perhaps, our society and its laws are making less and less distinction between marriage and living together. If society does still value marriage, it is doing precious little to prove it – and I am afraid the same goes for the churches. Roman Catholics are now as liable to get divorced as any other section of the community, and there is something of a panic on to see that young couples are adequately prepared for marriage. But the fact is, unless they are already serious members of their churches, couples are unlikely to turn to them for guidance.

As I have said before, I am reluctant to moralize about divorce because I think those involved undergo quite enough private suffering of their own. But I am a believer in old-fashioned Christian marriage, for various practical as well as religious reasons: I think it is good for society that people should stand up and say publicly 'I, John, belong to Jean – I, Jean, belong to John'. I think it makes an alliance of families – and family back-up, enlisting two or three generations, is terribly important. And I think that solemnly to ritualize one's promises does concentrate the mind wonderfully. It is not a bad idea, either, to take the heat off the sex angle and widen the context a bit – not least, to include God.

A few days ago, a listener sent me a printed copy of a wedding address delivered by a Derbyshire clergyman eighty-two years ago, and I will quote from it: 'You have today pledged your *troth*. Troth is an old English word which means Faith or Truth; and faithfulness is the groundwork of a really Christian character. Without faithfulness there can be no lasting happiness. Many people are very loving and bright when all things go smoothly . . . but when shadows come, and days are dark and dreary, they become peevish and fretful. But this is not *faithful* love.'

Humdrum sentiments, I suppose, but they had a special appeal to me. For the bride's father was the Reverend Edward Priestland – my grandfather, whom I never knew.

* *Living Together* is published by Hamlyn Paperbacks at £1.50.

Hoyle's Intelligence

16 January 1982

The scandal of the week, for ecclesiastical people, must be the news that an Englishwoman, ordained as an Anglican priest in the United States, has been celebrating illicit eucharists in this country, thereby calling down the wrath of the Bishop of London. Caviar to the general, I am afraid, though I only wish caviar would become as commonplace as (I suspect) women priests will be before this decade is out. In the meantime, there will be all sorts of cloak-and-dagger goings-on – nothing quite like it since the days of witchcraft and priest-holes.

For the general – that is, the general public – I would like to draw attention to a lecture by the astronomer Sir Fred Hoyle, given at the Royal Institution this week and sponsored by the American science magazine *Omni.* What was said has to be heard in the context of the current battle between Creationists and Evolutionists; though I fancy it will shock the fundamentalists in both camps.

Fred Hoyle believes that life came to Earth from outer space – indeed, that it is still reaching us in the form of immensely tough micro-organisms. He demonstrates that the chances of life developing here accidentally, out of that famous organic soup, are too remote to be taken seriously. He compares them to the chances of rolling an unbroken sequence of five million sixes with dice.

Next, Hoyle believes that the Darwinian theory of natural selection cannot explain the evolution which we know has occurred. The fossil evidence does not support it. Where *are* those famous missing links? Sir Fred argues that random mutations are too slow and anyway more likely to be harmful than beneficial. What he thinks happened is that viruses invaded the existing cells and triggered off dormant genes which had not been used before – causing the plant or animal to make an instant jump in behaviour. Thus the jump is triggered from outside, not inside, the organism. It is, in that sense, 'created'. All natural selection does is to accept the jump that fits the local environment.

Sir Fred believes that just as life is cosmic (that is, from beyond the Earth) so is intelligence. The difference between intelligent ordering and random shuffling is far too large to be ignored. Echoing the classic Argument from Design, Hoyle concludes that the materials of life, with their amazing and complex order, cannot be accidental but must be the outcome of intelligent design. Here he defines an intelligence as 'a huge store of information', and the human self as 'the software within the hardware of our bodies', adding that we have the instinctive feeling that our software might have an existence independent of our hardware (our bodies).

But why should Hoyle's Cosmic Intelligence want to create organic life? – as a matter of stark necessity, he suggests. He proposes that the Intelligence found itself being squeezed out of an unfavourable environment; so that it put together, as a deliberate act of creation, a new structure of life that enormously exceeded anything that could have arisen by accident.

Hoyle admits that here he is virtually talking about God; though he realizes it is an immanent rather than transcendent God – that is, a God within the Universe rather than outside it. And it is a God with certain weaknesses (which is an idea you can find in modern theology). However, in its struggle to perpetuate itself, the Cosmic Intelligence that preceded us has built into us the instruction: 'You are derived from something out there in the sky. Seek it and you will find much more than you expect.'

And this, says Fred Hoyle, is the foundation of the religious instinct that Man alone possesses and which he is constantly thrusting forward. 'We are the intelligence that preceded us in its new material representation. Or rather, we are the beginning of the re-emergence of that intelligence.'

Mummified Mumbo Jumbo

23 January 1982

Back in 1945, a couple of Egyptian peasants, digging for manure, unearthed a collection of fourth-century Coptic manuscripts of a type generally known as 'Gnostic'. Gnosticism goes back to pre-Christian times, and the essence of it is – if it is possible to condense such a cloudy tradition into a phrase or two – that the knowledge of God can never be for the vulgar, but is to be found in secret wisdom passed on from one initiate to another. Things are never what they seem: behind each appearance lies another ghostly truth and another. The Creator God – the Demiurge – was himself created. Jesus was not really man, nor did he really die on the Cross. He was the Lord of the Dance. Behind his public teaching lay a mysterious secret doctrine.

Some of these ideas have come down to us from other sources – the Koran, for example, insists that it was not Jesus who was crucified but someone else. It has taken more than thirty years for the 1945 Gnostic Gospels to filter down through the world of scholarship to that of popular journalism and do-it-yourself theology, where they are now providing all kinds of stimulation to the fantasies of those who will always accept the conspiracy theory of anything. True enough, orthodoxy – like history – gets written by the winning side: but the winning side is not necessarily wrong, and if you read the Gnostic Gospels for a day or two, you end up feeling that the Church did us and God a service by putting them out of circulation. It is curious that modern authors can be so sceptical of the standard Bible, and fall so easily for the confusion of the Gnostics.

Which brings me to the book in question this week: *The Holy Blood and The Holy Grail* by Henry Lincoln and two others. Anyone who believes that Bacon wrote Shakespeare, that Lee Harvey Oswald did not kill Kennedy, and that Hitler is alive and well and living in Venezuela will wallow happily in it – for it is all good, murky esoteric fun, woven of Gnosticism, rosicrucianism, cabalism and masonic mumbo jumbo, courtesy of Leonardo da Vinci, Isaac Newton, Victor Hugo and Claud (*L'après-midi d'un*

Faune) Debussy. The implication is that the mummified corpse of Jesus Christ lies in a subterranean vault beneath a lake in southern France, guarded by a secret society – an offshoot of the heretical Knights Templar – called the Priory of Sion. The time is drawing near when the Priory will reveal its secret, take over the Church and restore the earthly monarchy which was Jesus's real purpose.

For not only did Jesus not die on the Cross: he had children by Mary Magdalene, children who married into the royal families of Europe. The Sangraal was *not* the Holy Grail, it was the Sang Réal, the Royal Blood. So stand by for the Second Coming in the shape of – who? Dr Otto von Habsburg, MEP? The authors never even got round to ringing him up, apparently. Maybe it is even one of our own dear Stuarts, Sinclairs or Devonshires.

Of course it is not enough to cry 'Blasphemous heresy!' But if such a book had to be written, one would have hoped for rather more in the way of credentials on the part of the authors; and rather less in the way of 'If, as we assume . . . it might well have been . . .' The whole thing is full of unprovables and improbables. Is it really likely that Jesus could have survived the Cross for twelve years and been kept a secret? That St Paul – who is brushed aside here – could have investigated the early Church and cynically have thrown in his lot with a lie? That the Priory's secret (if there is one) would not have been blown long ago? In any case, Christians have nothing to fear, for it is not who Jesus *was* that matters to us – it is what we know he *is*, and if there is a mummy under a lake, it has nothing to do with that.

Anyhow, as a fellow journalist, I congratulate the authors on all their hard work in compiling this entertaining thriller.

Prophecy

30 January 1982

I'll tell you one of the most dangerous things about this job – and that is, the constant temptation to prophesy. There's an ambiguity in that word between its meaning as 'foretelling' and as 'forth-telling' – between clairvoyance of things to come and commentary on things present. I have little use and no talent for the former (which I'd call a distraction of the Devil, if I believed in him). But what opportunities I have for the latter: to demand this or denounce that, in the name of the Lord God Almighty!

One is urged to speak forth, not so much on behalf of various causes as against their opponents. Naturally, those who do the urging are already convinced of their own rightness; but they are even more keen to hear those who do not agree with them put down than they are to hear themselves exalted. I suppose that is because those who already believe they have the right answer want to be assured of it by hearing no other voice on the opposite side. There is a fear of genuine, calm disagreement, and an almost magical conviction that denouncing something – which is not an act, but only a formula of words – has value in itself. For example, rape is wrong, evil, degrading, illegal – anything you like to call it – and we all know that. But there is a temptation to prophesy against it, as if something were thereby achieved. Is it really much more than a gesture saying, 'I've said I'd hang the lot of them – so I'm in the clear'? In fact, many proposals for action are little more than gestures of denunciation.

The prophet in Old Testament times had the advantage

of complete independence. He was a spiritual freelance who claimed to speak only for the Will of God: nobody elected him, appointed or paid him, and you do not have many people like that around today. What's more, if you did have them the people the prophets denounced would either sue them or demand equal time for reply. The principle of balance and the fear of litigation are built into the traditions (and to a large extent the laws) of our society. Jeremiah and Ezekiel would never have got away with it today.

So we are trapped between being fair and being right. It seems to me that there are a number of things caught up in the issues of rape, railway strikes, the ban on women priests, the conduct of the media, and nuclear weapons, which are just plain wrong. But the sad thing about many of the campaigns over these issues is that they start from the assumption that 'the other side' is both inhuman and irrational and ought to be silenced or crushed.

Working as a journalist, one learns that both sides in any confrontation are human and have their reasons – though their different circumstances emphasize different human qualities. One side is often on the way up (because of those circumstances), but can't resist kicking the other, which is fighting for survival.

Another difficulty for the reporter is that often he cannot tell the public the full truth because (a) the Law prevents him, (b) an excited public doesn't want to believe it, (c) the reporter himself doesn't have the time to find out or explain it, and (d) those who know the truth won't tell it. There is much posturing, little openness, and time and again one surveys the tapestry of media coverage and exclaims, 'But that's not what it's really about! That isn't the real story!' (which is usually much more complex).

What prophets seldom do is urge people to value the

good qualities in one another, and respond to those. It is remarkable, in spite of the temptations, frustrations and provocations of the outrageous life we all lead, how good the average citizen is – how hardworking, orderly and humane, if only his fellow citizens will believe it of others (and not just of themselves) and call it out of them. After all – as Christians believe – God put it there.

He That Blasphemeth

6 February 1982

Blasphemy is my theme, though it may not be what you think. The definition approved by the courts is 'any contemptuous, reviling, scurrilous or ludicrous matter relating to God, Jesus Christ, or the Bible, or the formularies of the Church of England as by law established'. Blasphemy is a Common Law, that is, a traditional or judge-made offence. It has never been spelt out by Act of Parliament. As you will have noticed it is only the Christian religion, as defined by the Church of England, that is protected. The faiths of our Jewish, Muslim and Hindu fellow citizens enjoy no such privilege. (Not that the law has actually been applied more than a handful of times during this century.)

Which is why the Law Commission – whose job it is to revise and update the laws of the land – has been inviting the comments of anyone interested upon the question 'Should the present Common Law crime of blasphemy be kept, abolished, or replaced by a more precisely codified crime?' The Commission has had a great many letters about irreverence on television (which is not really the point), but very little on the central issue of whether it should be a statutory crime to injure people's religious feelings.

The Archbishop of Canterbury thinks it should be; and he wants to protect all religious groups – Christian or otherwise. Many other countries operate such laws, and it is surely not tyrannical to discourage rudeness. The Law Commission's provisional view is that the crime of blasphemy should be abolished and not replaced, but that there is need for a new law penalizing offensive behaviour in any place of worship, including synagogues, mosques and temples which, it seems, are not adequately protected by the law as it stands.

The Commission has thought extremely hard about this (unlike most of us) and I will try to summarize its reasoning. Remember: it has to think in terms of workable law, and not just moral indignation.

The Commission points out that as things are, it is almost impossible to know in advance whether your words will be taken as blasphemous or not. That depends entirely upon the findings of a particular jury as to the *manner* of the alleged blasphemy, rather than its substance. Freedom of speech is never unlimited; it may have to give way if it can be shown (as it was in the case of incitement to racial hatred) that public order is in danger. But there seems to be no real threat to religious toleration in Britain; nor is there much evidence of a social problem comparable to pornography. Not many people would now claim (alas) that the Christian faith is holding up our society.

It is hard enough to demonstrate the degree of hurt to anyone's feelings. Also, there is no agreement on what constitutes a religion. There are certain sects calling themselves religious, which many people would say deserve to be criticized and even condemned. So what with the difficulty of definition, the capriciousness of juries, the lack of use and the absence of any demonstrable threat to society, the Commission feels we can probably do without a law of blasphemy.

Many Christians will feel uncomfortable about this. They may or may not wish that the law was used more often; but without it, they suspect the floodgates (already leaking) would burst wide open. But what about other religions? It sounds reasonable to extend the law to them, but consider: it offends Hindu religious feelings to kill a cow; riots broke out in Pakistan once, because a foreigner called his dog Mohammed. Come to that, I once knew a basset hound called Moses. Should these be crimes? Anyone in my job knows there is hardly anything you can say that doesn't offend some religious group. Maybe a jury could draw the line between sober comment and deliberate insult. But the Law Commission fears that any new law would be deliberately flouted by people who wanted to become martyrs in the cause of free speech. It might equally be exploited by those who wanted to make us all pious by an Act of Parliament.

Uncomfortable Words

13 February 1982

'The Church of England seems uncertain about unity and unsure of itself in mission.' Not my words, but those of the anonymous writer of the preface to this year's *Church of England Year Book*. His observations are, in part, a reaction against last year's 'springtime of the Church' optimism; for this year's writer has a number of things to feel uncomfortable about.

For a start, he notes resentment among Conservatives in Parliament that, as one of them put it, 'the bishops of the Anglican Church seem more concerned with promoting vague social issues instead of insisting on personal holiness and high standards of personal conduct', and that the Church of England is looking more and more like the SDP at prayer. Facile, but not without a grain of truth (thinks the preface writer), and relations were not improved when both houses of Parliament started leaping to the defence of the 1662 Prayer Book and there were demands in the General Synod for Disestablishment.

Then there was the 'Partners in Mission' enterprise, in which seventeen overseas churchmen – heavily outnumbered by seventy from Britain – attempted a radical criticism of the Church of England and got no more than half-an-inch deep. It was, said one official, like being bombarded by a peashooter. It is easy enough to say that the C. of E. is too preoccupied with pastoral care, too little with evangelism. But where does it go from there? It certainly doesn't know itself, and it seems nobody else will tell it.

Does it embrace the Free Churches, in the Covenant for Unity? The preface writer thinks the wider ecumenical outlook is bleak. The Roman Catholics are holding back from the British Council of Churches, the Council itself has chronic financial troubles, and the annual Week of Prayer for Christian Unity is becoming a wearisome ritual. As for the Covenant, there is growing opposition among the United Reformed Church to the acceptance of bishops; while for some Anglicans the call of Rome is so strong that they would abandon the Covenant forthwith. With the added boost of the Pope's visit and the final report of the Anglican/Roman Catholic Commission, Free Church people are beginning to fear that the General Synod will draw back yet again. The preface writer himself tries to discourage hopes of re-negotiation and calls for a clear Yes or No to the Covenant.

And so we come to the papal visit. If John Paul wanted to

be Machiavellian, the best way of killing the Covenant would be to make concessions to the Church of England – for example, by admitting that Anglicans are valid priests and allowing Romans and Anglicans to share each other's Holy Communion. Offered such inducements, many Anglican priests, at least, would find it hard to keep their minds on Methodist and URC charms. But I must say, given centuries of papal authority on these matters, I find it very hard to see how the Pope *could* make such concessions. I agree with the preface writer that nobody should expect too much of this visit. Something harmonious about the role of the churches in the struggle for world peace, perhaps, but not a great deal more. Apart from anything else, it is going to be very difficult for this Pope – with his Polish background – to comprehend the nature of a church which is historically national, insists it is catholic and apostolic, but is not in communion with him and permits the widest of theological speculation within its ranks.

To master this will call for a great effort of imagination and tact. As the preface remarks, 'It would be an ecumenical disaster if the visit were to bring to a ferment the anti-Roman feeling which lies not far below the surface in many people.' If I may say so, it calls for equal tact and imagination from those very Protestants. If they really believe that they hold the truth, and that 'the Bishop of Rome hath no jurisdiction in this realm of England', then they have nothing to fear in letting him have his say, and everything to gain from plain good manners.

Pope's Hopes

20 February 1982

Was there a danger, asked the lady reporter from America, that the Pope's visit to Britain might bring out anti-Catholic feelings? 'There is, yes', answered Cardinal Hume. 'Have you any suggestions to offset it?'

This week's press conference about plans for the visit – still 'very fluid' in their thirty-seventh draft – indicated that the Cardinal's own strategy for countering strident Protestantism is to pray and bear it. 'This country has a complex history and it's a miracle he's coming here at all', said Father Basil. 'We Catholics love our Church and our country, so the Holy Father visiting the Queen involves us at a very deep level. But he's not coming to chuck his weight about. It is a pastoral visit, to help us renew our faith, to further the task of unity among all Christians, and to raise the hearts of the whole people to ideals that lie beyond the purely material.' The Cardinal did concede, though, that John Paul would probably have to say some 'hard things' to all concerned.

The framework of the journey – London, Canterbury, Coventry, Liverpool, Manchester, York, Edinburgh, Glasgow, Cardiff in barely six days – involves seven major events, each celebrating one of the seven sacraments – Confession and Matrimony rather obliquely because they are much too delicate to expose on television. Incidentally, the usual 'Popemobile' has been harshly renamed the SPT or 'Special Papal Transport'.

Without question the most intriguing aspect of the visit for non-Romans will be the Pope's encounter, at Canterbury, with the Archbishop of Canterbury and a delegation of Free Church leaders: they will have some two hours at their disposal for a round-table discussion of church unity, and individual chats at a stand-up, fork-in-hand luncheon (or maybe in some cases it will be a very long spoon). Father Basil urged, 'It would be unwise in my view to expect any sudden and dramatic change as a result of a one-day visit. We are dealing with organic growth – not a merger that can be accomplished with signatures to a document. I have told the other church leaders it would be unrealistic to expect a man undergoing this kind of programme to discuss highly controversial church issues. How far he is prepared to go is up to the Pope. But it calls for delicacy and tact on the part of the others. One hopes for a breaking down of prejudices and fears which might lead to further discussions in another situation.'

On the specifically Anglican question of when the final report of the Joint Anglican/Roman Catholic Commission can be expected, the Cardinal hoped some time in March. The report has been long delayed, and there are rumours that the Vatican is trying to add reservations to it. Father Basil observed that the theologians had done their work – and now it was up to the churches to study, reflect, and decide whether to make it their own. Evidently there will be no great hurry about this. The Anglicans, being a world-wide communion, cannot give final judgement before the next Lambeth Conference in 1988; and Rome, said the Cardinal, would need a comparable period. The Pope's visit would launch everyone purposefully on that reflective stage: what lay beyond that was a secret of the Holy Spirit.

It seemed to me that Father Basil also raised a warning flag to the liberals in his own church. 'Renewal', he said, was a word somewhat misused. It did not simply mean changing things in the Church (though things might have to be changed). It should not mean making things easier – for renewal, people often had to be more disciplined. Watch out for 'hard things'!

But, said the Cardinal, the appeal of the Pope reached beyond his own Roman Catholic community, to those who embraced other faiths or none in particular. He had much to say about God and about man which was vital to the well-being of Society as a whole. The coming Lent would be a period of spiritual preparation for the visit, and Roman Catholics would welcome the co-operation of other local churches in it.

Owzat?

6 March 1982

It is one of Fate's craziest jokes that a great moral issue should have been presented to the nation in the shape of a game of cricket. Among reasonable people there can be little disagreement, I'm sure, that of all the ways that men (though, significantly, few women) have devised for passing the time between meals, cricket is by far the most vacantly silly, self-defeating and boring. How it still qualifies as a sport beats me – perhaps the truth is that it doesn't: it is now a cross between a gainful form of employment, an extension of cold warfare, and a device for preventing the Third Programme from playing the classical music it was designed to play – which shows how far cricket has strayed from the original idea of providing some innocent physical fun for children great and small (something that baseball still contrives to do, and what is more, in a finite time and with no damage to international relations).

But *is* the fact that a dozen professional cricketers have

been hired to practise their craft in South Africa really a moral issue at all? Or is it just politics? The players themselves would probably tell us they are not interested in politics at all, and the South African authorities would murmur approval in the background: it is just a game, they would say. But is it? Black and brown cricketing countries do not seem to agree – any more than certain white countries agreed that the Moscow Olympics were just the Games. If I were President Brezhnev or Mr Botha, I should be very keen to demonstrate that ordinary sporting chaps regarded my country as perfectly normal, nothing to make a fuss about. Like it or not – and I do not like it – sport has been *made* an instrument of politics. The competitor who insists otherwise cannot thereby undo the political consequences of his action.

Matters get more complicated still when a non-totalitarian state like Britain gets involved. The individual has a right to travel and practise his trade abroad. Teams representing Britain are not under state command (though that day might come, I suppose). Just how far can the State go in leaning on individuals in the national interest?

Then there is the question of hypocrisy. If we should not play games with countries whose governments do unpleasant things to their people, where do we stop? Do we stop at games – and go on trading and maintaining diplomatic contacts? Do we stop at South Africa – and keep normal relations with communist countries which oppress dissidents, and India, where untouchables are regularly murdered by caste Hindus? There is one important distinction to be made here, by the way: while apartheid is explicitly law in South Africa, caste discrimination is explicitly outlawed in India – it may be tenacious, but it is illegal; you must blame certain people for it, rather than the government.

But hypocrisy is a blunt and deadening word. There is good, scriptural authority for telling people to take the beam out of their own eye before pointing to the mote in their brother's. But if we embark on the course of saying, 'You are a hypocrite for demonstrating against apartheid while there is still racial discrimination in London' or – more dodgily – 'The campaign against the English cricketers is just a load of black racism' – we end up boycotting everything, or tolerating everything. The world is now full of moral issues, prowling about, seeking whom they may devour. It seems to me important that the religious person should seek to know, through prayer, those which he or she is called upon to adopt effectively; and those which most of us can affect are usually under our noses.

And I suppose you might say that apartheid is now under the noses of the English cricketers: that it is up to them now to communicate what they feel about it to the South Africans they meet. The same was said about going to the Moscow Olympics, but I do not think it ever stood a hope. All through life good people – especially when they have 'star appeal' – get manipulated, even when they think they are exercising their own free will. Read 'The Temptations in the Wilderness'.

A Transient Short-range Programme

13 March 1982

This is a transient short-range programme – and I claim the prize of a guided cruise for two to the target of my choice, for saying so. That terminal excursion (presumably strapped to the back of a Cruise Missile) is the reward offered for being the first person to get published a hitherto unused bit of gobbledygook from *The Strategic Phrase Fabricator.* This consists of three concentric cardboard wheels – each with a series of pompous words on it – which you shift around to produce endless permutations of important-sounding verbiage. Of all unexpected sources, the Fabricator is fabricated by the Peace-making campaign of the Scottish Episcopal Church at the Cathedral Office in Dundee. They'll send you one for fifty pence.

The instructions on the back invite you to dial ten random phrases and then ask yourself if you understand them. Let's see: 'a flexible pluralistic dialogue', 'a meaningful preventive consensus', 'a comprehensive pressurized capability', 'a normative rationalized deterrent' – it all sounds like good, convincing Haig-speak. If you have actually used more than half of them in conversation, the Fabricator identifies you as 'probably a Presidential speech-writer' or 'definitely in line for a Cabinet post'. If you cannot make head or tail of Haig-speak, the Fabricator reveals its true colours: 'Congratulations!' it says. 'Carry on demanding definitions whenever you hear these phrases used.'

Having worked in the United States – where, of course, Haig-speak comes from – I know there is more tnan a touch of transatlantic leg-pulling about the Fabricator. American defence officials really do use language awfully like that, and I have always put it down to the fact that there is far more of the German in their cultural make-up than we (the British) like to imagine. Translate those phrases into German, and they would sound perfectly natural. American defence planners approach their work with the same high seriousness as a German scientist or – come to that – theologian. (One could, without much difficulty, assemble an equally convincing Theological Phrase Fabricator, turning out concepts like 'a transcendent apophatic revelation' or 'a dogmatic eschatological ontology'.) It is said that such phrases are short-hand for something even more complicated; which is not always true, since they can often be reduced to something terrifyingly simple like 'Everyone will be dead, I'm afraid' or 'God is Love'. Their essential purpose is to show that the speaker is a member of the club, having attended the right seminars and read the right books. Thus he is a cool professional, not one of those woolly and emotional amateurs.

In my experience, the British – both military men and theologians – are actually a good deal less prone to Haig-speak than our friends and allies, as a result of which those friends and allies tend to regard both our theologians and our military men as being somewhat less than serious – which is a pity. It is foolish to pretend that all great ideas are simple – and dangerous to oversimplify them – but if an idea is clear in the head of the thinker, it *can* be expressed with clarity. The importance of this in defence matters – when the citizen has a right to know what is being done in his defence – is obvious. Clear speaking in religious matters seems to me just as important.

It cannot be said often enough that faith is not just a matter of argument – that heart and guts are involved, as well as head. But the secular world prides itself upon reasoned argument, and if the world of faith does not join in and make its case in terms the rest can understand, then faith will get brushed aside as an optional hobby for those whose minds have gone soft. That is one very simple case for abandoning Holy-speak and using services in modern English, or writing theology for the layman: it challenges us to ask ourselves, 'Do we really mean this? Are we just showing we are members of the club? And if we do mean it, how do we defend and develop it?' It is no use spinning the wheels for another phrase of jargon.

Orange, Red and Blue

20 March 1982

My notebook for the past week is unusually full of jottings – beginning with a reference back to the previous week's disgraceful (and I would say sacrilegious) demonstrations against the Archbishops of Liverpool and Canterbury; protests against the forthcoming visit of the Pope. If anyone crudely imagines that the Church of England is about to be sold to Rome, they show little understanding of how far there is still to go along the ecumenical road anyway, of how the churches of Rome and Canterbury are actually governed, and of the inevitable interest of Parliament in such matters. Perhaps it is no bad thing that we should be made to debate what kind of church we want: but let it be a civilized debate, and not a vulgar brawl.

On Tuesday, I found myself taking part in a Lent Course organized by BBC Radio Medway. First there was a talk,* then an interval for discussion by listening-groups, and finally a very tough 'phone-in, with some twenty callers demanding justification of what the speaker had said – which was very good for him. But I only mention it because it showed what the churches – who organized and staffed the programme, manned the 'phones and produced the literature – can do as a team in collaboration with their local radio station. Medway is not the only one, by any means, but it is an excellent example of how lay people, as well as clergy, can develop the ministry of the air.

Wednesday's newspapers brought two pauses for thought. The first was a speech by Mr Tony Benn, headlined in the *Guardian* BENN'S MARXIST FAITH. I am hardly qualified to discuss here his statements about the political treatment of Marxism, but there is one passage, reproduced identically in *The Times,* which is unquestionably a religious affair. Mr Benn, incidentally, has long taken an interest in early seventeenth-century religious-political groups like the Diggers and Levellers, and I think it is true to say that his socialism goes back to those roots – and before them, to the Lollards and the Peasants' Revolt – rather than to continental Marxism. Like it or not, his tradition is profoundly English and Puritan, to the scorn of some Marxists, who regard him as sentimental and isolationist.

What Mr Benn said was: 'Marxism is now a world faith, and must be allowed to enter into a continuous dialogue with other world faiths, including religious faith.' Shock! Horror! It looks as if Mr Benn was saying that Marxism is a religion, and ought to be treated like one by the others. But he was, in fact, making a distinction between faith and religious faith. You might argue that that is not strictly possible; and I have doubts myself, whether it is good Marxism to call Marxism a faith. It likes to think of itself as a science, which must stand or fall by its proofs. Faith stands on different foundations.

The dialogue that Mr Benn calls for has, indeed, been going on for some time – especially, as he knows, in Latin America. The trouble is, it always seems to be faith that has to end up giving ground – which is not surprising, since Marxism is specifically anti-religion and Marx himself was a radical atheist. I do not see how anyone can live in England and doubt the reality of class conflict and injustice. But no Christian can ever trust a philosophy that shuffles off sin onto systems, or which advocates hatred as constructive. Faith claims to judge all systems as its inferiors. On its own level, it admits no dual membership.

But Mr Benn's speech was unobtrusive compared with that big black half-page, paid for by the Police Federation, calling for the return of capital punishment. Britain might not be in the company of the most enlightened nations if she did restore hanging, and Christian opinion as a whole seems divided about capping every unnatural death with a second in the name of society. But Bible readers will know it is there in the Old Testament – as the penalty for blasphemy, adultery, homosexuality and striking or cursing a parent, as well as murder. And it is allowed by the Thirty-seventh of the Thirty-nine Articles.

* For the text, see page 216.

A Fearful Joy

27 March 1982

This is my two hundred and fiftieth talk in the series. No reason why it should be any different from the two hundred and forty-ninth, but I shall take it as an excuse for saying once more that the greatest privilege of the job is the conversation that has developed over the years with you, the listeners. I think I can say it has not just been me talking at you from the safety of the Broadcasting House basement, but a genuine two-way communication.

At times, it has overwhelmed me – there have been too many letters to answer. I am sure I deserve a certain amount of correction and I do my best to cope with would-be suicides and children who have run away to join the Moonies. But unsolicited manuscripts – usually without return postage – have become something of a burden; I now have eight copies of a small blue book called *Truth*, denouncing Easter as obnoxious to God; and more than enough pamphlets identifying the Pope with something nasty in the Book of Revelation.

But from time to time there comes a rare reward. For example, a letter that came the other day from a retired Cornish mining engineer in which he describes a classic case of direct experience of God. He writes to me: 'I am no plaster saint. I live very much in the world. But what I have told you now is the first time I have ever told anybody . . .' I was able to write back, assuring him that even his reticence was typical of something which is far more common than most people suppose. Quoting his letter, this is how it happened one afternoon thirty-four years ago: 'I suppose I had nodded off. For I woke up with the sun streaming down on my face – just enjoying doing nothing in particular, listening to the birds singing. Suddenly, I became aware of a strange mixture of fear and uplift entering my mind, and sat there deeply puzzled for some minutes. Finally, it became so insistent that I had to find out what it meant.

'I walked up the passage to my bedroom, went down on my knees, and asked. As I did so, the Glory of the Universe shone before me. I was blinded by the dazzling white light. In my heart, I flung my arms before my eyes, because I knew that man could not look upon God and live. I was both terrified and yet uplifted – I can't explain it – I was shattered. And then I knew that I was a nothing. All my conceit and personal esteem vanished.'

The letter continues: 'So great and awful was the Holiness that stood before me that I feared lest it should ever happen again. But it completely changed my life. When I hear men in their folly say, "You can't prove that there is a God", I reply, "You wait until he takes half a step towards you, and you are left in no doubt."

'Why this happened to me', writes my correspondent, 'I

cannot understand. It may have been to arm and stiffen me for what was coming: for my world was about to collapse about my ears.' He then describes the sudden death of his father and the long, painful death of his mother, from which he emerged with what he calls 'the inner revelation of the fact of personal resurrection' which has left him 'doing my best to bring comfort to those who are breaking their hearts over the bodily death of their loved ones'.

To people like my correspondent – and, as I say, he is far from being unique – such experiences are incapable of being explained away. They weren't fasting or taking drugs or working themselves into a state of ecstasy or in any sense looking for such an experience. But when it came, it was a *total* experience of the whole being – far more real than everyday reality. And, as a final test, it transforms the rest of their lives – though, typically, they tell no one else about it, and cannot understand why they should have been chosen for it. Says my correspondent: 'The abiding realities are things which we cannot experience with our senses – but they are real enough. We need to live like a man astride of two worlds. We are here for the time being, and have a duty to live accordingly; but we ought never to forget that the permanent one is only just around the corner.'

ARCIC Explorers

3 April 1982

POPE TO RULE CHURCH OF ENGLAND said one headline I saw, announcing the final report of the Anglican/Roman Catholic International Commission – hereinafter known as ARCIC. But it really is not as simple as that.

After some fifteen years' work, a group of theologians

from England, Ireland, Australia and North America has worked out a joint theory of the Church, on the basis of which it thinks the two great Christian families could re-unite; and the central feature of this theory is that the world-wide Church *needs* an earthly leader, and that no one is better suited to be this Universal Primate (as ARCIC calls him) than the Bishop of Rome. Whether or not you think Our Lord's references to St Peter were meant to apply to all Peter's successors (and ARCIC has doubts about that) the historical fact is, it says, that the Bishop of Rome did emerge as supreme, or at least 'first among equals'. Yes, there have been some rotten popes, as there have been rotten kings, revolutionaries and elected moderators. But the providential action of the Holy Spirit has been at work in the office of the papacy.

There are two assumptions without which the Anglicans and Roman Catholics could not even have begun work. The first is the assumption that the Christian Church is above national boundaries. So no offence meant to the Queen, who is formally – though hardly actively – Supreme Governor of the Church of England. Already, a large part of the Anglican Church (in America, for example) owes her no allegiance. The second assumption, a theological one, concerns the sacramental and apostolic nature of the Church – the continuous handing down of the Holy Communion (and its deepest meanings), of the ordained ministry that serves it, and of the episcopacy that governs it. If you cannot share these assumptions – as Anglicans and Roman Catholics largely do – then you cannot really join in ARCIC's game at all.

It is by no means simple if you do stay in. The kind of pope envisaged by ARCIC is one who *could* exist, under the reforms of Vatican Two, but does not exist yet: one who acts almost as Mr Speaker to a House of Bishops. An ideal job, one day, perhaps, for Cardinal Hume . . . However, we are told, 'Primacy is not an autocratic power . . . The Universal Primate should exercise his ministry in association with his brother bishops . . .' Yet we are also told, 'He has the right to intervene in the affairs of a diocese . . . The diocesan bishop is subject to his authority.'

The report notes that Anglicans are entitled to an assurance that acknowledging the primacy of the Pope would not involve the suppression of their traditions and the imposing of alien ones. ARCIC thinks that, in effect, they already have such an undertaking. But I imagine that Parliament, public and General Synod would want to see that in very clear black and white. For – don't forget – Parliament still sees itself as the guardian of the Book of Common Prayer and the Thirty-nine Articles, which declare 'The Bishop of Rome hath no jurisdiction in this realm of England'. And there are still many English Christians – Free Church and Anglicans – who do not regard the Reformation as a misunderstanding that is best forgotten, but as a stand for truth *never* to be forgotten.

ARCIC slides delicately round the topic of women priests, as I am quite sure the Vatican will not. ARCIC has nothing to say about divorce and contraception, on which Roman Catholics, like Anglicans, are listening to their own consciences these days, anyway. It hopes Anglicans will not be required to subscribe to the dogmas about the Virgin, though it thinks a lot too much fuss has been made over these. And it ties itself in terrible knots over Papal Infallibility. He *can* be wrong, it says, and he *can* be right, but under very special conditions, and it has all been exaggerated, and anyway 'positions are not static'. Back in Rome, hints have already been dropped that they jolly well are; I suspect the ARCIC report is being passed from cardinal to cardinal like a lewd novel.

Here in England, perhaps, minds are broader on both sides. But it is still going to take many years for church governments and church people to figure it all out. So plenty of debate, please, but no panic.

Easter Even

10 April 1982

This day – Easter Even, as the Prayer Book calls it – has an empty, dead feel about it: suspended between the tragedy of Crucifixion and the triumph of Resurrection. It is a day, surely, when Christians ought to stay indoors. For the past week has been almost too much, and what happened yesterday was the end of all our hopes – or so it seemed. He descended into Hell . . . Not quite the place of eternal punishment, I think; more of a Limbo, or the ancient Hebrew *Sheol*, where the souls of those who had died before Christ slept uneasily, awaiting his coming to judge them. A friend of mine suggested the dramatic scene of the arrival there of the hanged Judas Iscariot – to find the gates burst open, and the Lord whom he had betrayed confronting him. Judas, of all the disciples, the first to know the real truth . . .

But this is rather a mediaeval fantasy. It is hard to be sure what the earliest churches thought about the descent into Hell; though there is certainly a version of it in Chapter 3 of the First Epistle of Peter: 'He went and preached unto the spirits in prison, which sometimes were disobedient . . .' Though it sounds as if these were demons rather than human souls. The descent into Hell doesn't appear in the creeds before the fourth century. So I am afraid I have to look elsewhere for a thought to fill Easter Even.

What must have struck so many of Jesus's followers on that day of utter defeat was the weakness of God – his powerlessness to save his own son. It certainly had occurred to those who mocked him, as he hung dying on the Cross. What happened on Easter morning was to teach them all a lesson, of course; crucifixion was only half the story: but I am sure it is no accident that the scene which puts the whole Christian faith into one frozen frame is that of the Cross, not the empty tomb. That emptiness has to be filled by faith – or else by a variety of heretical theories. Far more of a fact is the nailing up of Christ upon the Cross.

What does it mean? I think, myself, that the power of the Cross is partly due to the fact that it is at the crossing of many different meanings, which speak to different people in different circumstances at different times. The same, I think, is true of the Eucharist – that other central act of the faith; and the power of both is diminished when we try to knock out meanings and leave only one which is claimed as the truth.

The meaning which I find speaks loudly to many Christians today is precisely that of the Cross as a sign of the weakness of God. I think it is certainly there in the Gospel, as it must always be, but I think it is drawn out for us today because it accords with what we see about us: the poor children of God suffering, the wicked and well-to-do triumphing, goodness mocked, brutality exalted. So while the Cross may very well be a sacrifice for the sins of the world, if you will, it can also be seen as a sign of the way God is: 'I am like this. I am like you. I am *so* like you that I also suffer and die – to rise again.'

The weakness of God – the limitation of his power – is there in the Bible from the very start: when he creates a world not of his own whims and fancies, but of order which he does not keep tinkering with. He weakens himself still further when he gives Man and Woman the power of moral choice: the power to frustrate his design by deciding they know better. Of course, they have also the power to work *with* that design – in which case, God's love becomes almighty indeed, because we recognize and return it. If we fail to recognize it and reject it, then he is weak. The love still hangs there, bleeding, but there is no response to it and it descends into Hell.

To rise again! Whatever it was that happened at Easter, the point is that the risen Christ was recognized by men and women, who saw that his power lay not in any kind of force, but in a love to be worked with. First they had to accept God's weakness, and out of it rose his power.

No Island is a Man

17 April 1982

When news came of the invasion of the Falklands, I was in Rome: luckily, because if I had been near a microphone in London I should probably have got the sack. Superficially, there were so many ludicrous aspects – including the image of all those grand persons running around in their underwear. And then pulling the gunboats out of hock – to go *where*? against *whom*? It couldn't be true! But as the realization dawned that it was, and the language of 1956 came back on the air, a mixture of pacifism and memories of being a foreign correspondent rose to the surface, crying 'But this is wrong! And win or lose, it's a disaster for us!' As I say, luckily I never did get such treason on the air – the opinion polls suggest it represents only an unmanly minority – and what follows will be a carefully balanced piece, putting both sides of the case and cancelling itself out.

With a few exceptions like Lord Soper, Dr Kenneth Greet and Sir Stanley Meyer MP, there have been few voices raised to renounce the use of force. This, I think, shows that when it comes to live issues involving one's own country and its dignity, the Christian imperative for peace still finds it hard to stay on the road. After all, there are the Falkland islanders – our own kith and kin, put there on our behalf and doing nobody the slightest harm – and here comes an exceedingly nasty brutish regime to squat on them. Easy (even if true) to say that we should have got out from under the situation years ago, or been better prepared to resist: but here and now, is there any realistic chance of securing the islanders' freedom without being ready to use force? And it is fatuous to pretend such a show, unless it teeters on the brink of action.

Britain can cite international law, the United Nations Charter, the Security Council, the solidarity of most of our allies and even the Doctrine of the Just War in support of our rights. As the Christian politician Mr Enoch Powell pointed out – peaceful solutions to every problem cannot mean that every time the aggressor grabs what he wants, the victim must surrender at least half his rights. If that is what compromise means, then (as Mr Powell argued) the Charter of the United Nations has become the charter for pirates. It was Dr David Owen who pointed out that the original Charter envisaged a UN police force, intervening, if necessary. before aggression took place. But such powers do not exist. and perhaps the world should reproach itself for failing to let the UN grow up. As things are, it is not unreasonable in a world of sinful men to speculate about domino theories, about national honour and commitments, about not letting our boys down and (from a somewhat different angle) about the wisdom of selling arms to almost anyone who isn't a communist. That one has long worried the churches.

And yet, if it is possible to assert that most of these arguments are not contrary to the Gospel, and that the Christian is not called upon to go soft in the head when confronted with wickedness, can we at the same time maintain that it is the will of Christ that we set forth prepared to kill Argentinians? They started it (with minimal bloodshed, by the way). Do we, as Christians also, continue it therefore? And while we stand loyal to our government's honour and interests, is it necessary to forget that the other side believes that its honour and interests are equally at stake, and believes that very passionately? Dictatorship notwithstanding, the Argentinian people probably think they are as right as we think we are right.

Wailing and gnashing teeth won't help, though. I suppose many Christians will accept what they feel has to be done as the lesser of two evils, and perhaps beg forgiveness for the sins of the world which continue to hammer nails into the Cross. That should certainly be an element in our prayers for peace this Sunday. Anger and pride can corrupt judgement. Once violence is unleashed, it is very, very hard to know where it will end.

Jaw, War and the Pope

24 April 1982

As I record this, the penny is still spinning: heads for war, tails for peace. By the time you hear these words, I suppose the coin may be lying flat on the table for all to see, and it could make nonsense of everything I say. I should be glad if it did, for it is hard to be very comforting or cheerful at the moment.

I open one letter: 'They started it', it says. 'Aggression

must not pay.' I open another: 'This public glee sickens me', it says. 'Killing people is wrong.' If only it were so simple, either way. It is very hard, for example, not to feel pride in the behaviour of the Marines who defended South Georgia (and who killed people) – or, for that matter, not to acknowledge the gratuitous chivalry of repatriating them afterwards. If there is to be further fighting, let us hope that spirit – with its echoes of the better side of mediaeval Christendom – can be maintained. There used to be codes of warfare observed: they have slipped, most of all in this century.

Christians can be in no doubt that they ought to be praying at this time; but in so doing, they can lay themselves open to the ridicule of non-believers. Prayers for victory? Prayers for the safety of our warriors? But both sides are doing that! How does God decide which to favour? And if we win, does that mean British Protestant prayers are better than Argentine Catholic ones – that God's on our side (and tough luck on the Argentine lads who fell fighting for the wrong cause)? But that, surely, is to regard prayer as a kind of magic spell: say the right words and your wish is granted. It was, in fact, an English Catholic who said to me she could only imagine praying for those who were about to suffer on *both* sides, imploring God's forgiveness for the sinfulness of all mankind that had brought the blasphemy of war, and then (as she put it) 'listening like mad for guidance on how we can pick up the pieces and get some good out of the mess'. I would add, myself, that just as prayer for the sick can strengthen them – so we ought to be praying for our political leaders. It would be good to know that they, too, were opening themselves to the Spirit at this time.

There is some glee among anti-papists at the prospect that the crisis may cause the postponement of the visit to

Britain by the Pope – though if they see the Hand of the Lord in it, then surely God moves in a drastic, as well as a mysterious, way. In the meantime, leaflets circulate presenting the Pope as a personification of superhuman evil; and I have had two letters, gruesomely illustrated, threatening his life – both of which have been passed to the police.

A postponement of the visit would have nothing to do with Argentina's Roman Catholicism, though. To visit a country at war – or liable to become at war at any minute – would not only spoil the impact of the tour and make all the Pope's talk of peace and reconciliation sound futile; it would run the risk of plunging him into some episode – a victory, a defeat, an atrocity – of which the media and their cameras would make him a part, even if he pretended to ignore it; and could he? As a leader of Christianity world-wide, he cannot risk being compromised. The Vatican has diplomatic, as well as spiritual, intelligence enough to realize that.

Postponement would be a grave disappointment not only to British Roman Catholics, but to that part of the Church of England (in particular) which was hoping for a boost to reunion. Well, the chance would come again later; and it has to be said that there are moderate and progressive church people who would not mind a postponement; who would rather this year's debate about the Covenant for Unity among the non-Roman churches proceeded without the influence of a papal visit. I guess the security forces would heave a sigh of relief as well. But a battle for the Falklands is hardly the price anyone would have chosen to pay. Let's not pretend that war can be done without suspending some Christian values.

Living by the Sword

1 May 1982

War does simplify matters – while it lasts. Though war after war – even the war against Hitler – has shown that one set of intolerable injustices is usually replaced by another. The past month, however, has produced in most people the effect of a gathering thunderstorm: we would rather it broke and wreaked its havoc than went on splitting our heads with tension. Anyone who has tried following the arguments in Parliament, on television, in the press – unless he or she is unusually single-minded – must have despaired of finding any simple way through them. The arguments of law find their way blocked by the defects of enforcement. One man's sovereignty (and what *does* that word mean?) is another man's imperialism. We cut through one layer of history to another and another – each further from the reality of today than the last. Everybody's motives seem mixed. Who is telling the truth about what, and what is really going on? It is so tempting to cut the cackle and have a good bash, if only to break up the puzzle and start a new game. That, I think, is how a great many people feel, and the churches have not been able to do much to help them.

Earlier this week, the Baptist Union, meeting in London, passed a careful resolution expressing sympathy with the government in its dilemma, praying that peace with justice might prevail, and urging the withdrawal of the Argentine forces, the non-engagement of the British fleet, and United Nations responsibility until a diplomatic solution was reached. Fine in theory, and most of it in keeping with Resolution 502 of the Security Council: except that Britain does not trust Argentina, Argentina does not trust Britain, and there is little respect anywhere for a toothless United Nations.

It is this which has kept the wind out of the sails of most of the church appeals about the Falklands: they assume a motive-power which does not really exist. Cardinal Hume, on the other hand, has published an article in the Roman Catholic press indicating that, in the last resort, the Church could recognize Britain's claim to use military force in defence of her rights. He adds, 'The United Kingdom may well have an added responsibility to take action in so far as aggression often thrives on inaction and appeasement.'

The Cardinal is restating the ancient theory of the Just (or more properly, Justifiable) War. All other means of upholding one's legitimate rights must have been exhausted. There must be due proportion between the force used and the cause of the conflict. The 'lesser of two evils' argument has to bear in mind the dangers of escalation. Thus the Cardinal's statement does not necessarily imply a *carte blanche* for Britain's Task Force. One can still agonize about whether this *is* the very last resort; whether self-defence includes counter-offensive; and whether the dangers of escalation *are* under control. It may be that the answers to all these questions are reassuring, and that military theologians (if there is such a profession) will put this operation in the rare category of 'theologically respectable'; but again, perhaps not.

For one cannot help recalling, also, the words of the present Pope, in his first Encyclical. Having condemned the arms trade, and admitting he would be criticized for saying as much, he went on: 'The Church implores everybody, in the name of God and Man: Do not kill! Do not prepare destruction and extermination! Think of your brothers and sisters suffering hunger and misery! Respect each other's dignity and freedom!' The words of John Paul II; and no doubt they apply quite as much to the Argentine Junta as they do to us.

At least on the evidence of television, there seems to be nothing like the bellicosity in Britain that has exploded in Buenos Aires. The nearest I have had to jingoism came from a listener who wrote: 'Why should a Christian hesitate to fight when the Bible is full of warfare? Greater love hath no man than to lay down his life for his friends . . .' Well, yes, I agree. But it says nothing there about killing his enemies.

Just War

8 May 1982

It is not yet treason to express more than one side of a case, but if it were, the media would have to share a dungeon with the churches. Cardinal Hume, the Archbishop of Canterbury and the Bishop of London have justified the Falklands Expedition: the Bishop of Manchester, the Bishop of St Andrews and the Roman Catholic Bishop in East London have deplored it. Two former Anglican bishops in Argentina – Bishop Harris and Bishop Flagg – have reminded us there is Argentine patriotism as well as British patriotism. The fact is that church people are caught up in the same compromised world as the rest of us.

It seems to me there are three kinds of response to aggression. First, the pacifist position: that whatever the wrong done, violence is so evil and uncontrollable that it must never be added to by counter-violence; for the Christian has before him the example of halting evil by enduring it. Second, there is what you might call the commonsense reaction: that unless you are prepared to uphold your rights by force, force will become the only right. Finally, agonized between the two, there is the uncomfortable theory of the Just War. I have mentioned this before, and I think it is what this country aspires to; yet it is far from easy to apply, and theologians are finding it less and less tenable.

The early Church made a distinction between individuals, who had to love their enemies and turn the other cheek, and the State, which to preserve public order in a world corrupted by sin was obliged to use force in order to avenge and resist evil. Gradually it was developed that for war to be just, certain conditions had to be observed. War must be the last resort. The cause itself must be just. The intention of the campaign must be right and the hopes of success reasonable. The methods employed must be proportionate to the end. War must be *declared*, and by legitimate authority. And the good expected must be at least as great as the evil caused. Since killing people was so obviously against the Gospel, this theory did not claim to make war good, but only to restrict it to the minimum, the lesser evil.

Our government would surely claim to have respected the spirit of this. But wisdom after the event shows how hard it is to calculate the equations: is there no other resort? how reasonable is the hope of success? is the good to be expected as great as the evil which may arise, or the means proportionate to the end? For we are not living in a mediaeval world, where weapons are limited in effect and disruption confined to the battlefield. Weapons technology and mass communications have made it possible for a single shot to shake the world.

Had nuclear weapons been involved (as in a few years

they may be, even by a third-rate nation) then the effect would be even more shattering. There may not be many more chances to fight an old-fashioned war anywhere. Conscious of this, from the 1950s onwards, the Church has been cutting back the Just War theory in the direction of non-violence (to the alarm of many conventional politicians). The Church has not denied the right to self-defence, but it does not think that right is unlimited, and it has passionately denounced the arms race and the arms trade. It is hard to think of any branch of the Church which has not been urging, for years past, the subjection of sovereign national rights to the international community. Many states, like Argentina, have thought it a lesser evil to ignore that and fight for their own rights. This may be an opportunity for us all to think again.

Which is not to deny that in moral and legal terms Argentina has done wrong, or that Britain has tried to act justly. But until war is actually declared and censorship imposed, it cannot be disloyal to wonder if modern warfare *can* be kept in proportion, or if even the lesser evil is not too great. There is a reflection of this in the great tenderness of both sides over casualties.

Raw Nerves

15 May 1982

In view of my own convictions, which I've tried to counterbalance though not conceal, I had expected by now to be taking heavy incoming mortar-fire from some of my listeners. 'Dishonourable', 'odious' and 'subversive' would have done nicely. But it simply has not happened. I would not pretend that my mail-bag is a cross-section of public opinion: but the letters I have had over the past four weeks have been, almost without exception, out of sympathy with what our leaders have been doing with our ships and our boys.

I have the impression that had war been formally declared, with a national government, censorship and powers of direction over the mass media, some of my correspondents would have found their way clearer. It is the ambiguity between war and peace they find confusing. Christians, who expect to find a 'Christian answer', but still do not know what the question is, are finding it very difficult. For their own leaders are divided.

It is tempting to jump right in and have a bash, or at least to talk as if bashing were the patriotic thing to do, on the grounds that this will give heart to our boys and scare the wits out of those bean-eating Argies and their tin-pot dictator (I hope I have used the appropriate insults). But our government itself has refrained for weeks from all-out bashing. It has tried very hard to give talks a chance and not squander human life. If there has been torment for believers in non-violence and frustration for the advocates of force, there must have been unbearable tension for a cabinet juggling with both. It would be charitable to ascribe some of the accusations that have been flying about – especially against the media – to that tension. At times like these, everyone is so overwhelmed by the problems before them that they find it hard to envisage anybody else's and become resentful of anything but wholehearted sympathy and support. Even a glance at the other side of the case implies that *you* are not doing your best – which is cruel.

The media are conspicuous but (I think) relatively unimportant. It is unhealthy to become obsessed with them. The difficulties they are encountering, although mild in comparison with those of managing the crisis, frustrate the very purpose of their trade: which is to say what is going on. There is a score of journalists with the *Hermes* – all eager to deluge us with the doings of our boys – but handicapped by communications and security. It is hard for them to win a war which is not being fought, or to make propaganda when there is nothing available to propagate. And so we bring on the retired admirals and the far-from-reluctant partisan politicians. And something gets said – even a routine turn of phrase – which drops like acid on an exposed nerve.

No nerves can be more exposed than those of the relatives of our boys in the Task Force. Clever arguments about the rights and wrongs of sending them at all must seem – to those relatives – not just insulting but treacherous. As indeed it would be to their opposite numbers in a certain country where (as we have been reminded) the right to dissent does not exist. But that, I suppose, is one of the things we would be fighting for: the right to say that your government, if not your country, is wrong, and to prove or disprove it by publishing every fact you can legitimately get. The journalist's responsibility to do that is a much heavier one – with more far-reaching effects on the credibility of the media – than the sort of responsibility which implies embarrassing nobody.

The Christian message behind all this is that politicians, journalists, soldiers and relatives everywhere are levelled under the fatherhood of God. None should yield to the temptation to regard another as subhuman, or himself as superhuman. All are tainted with the sins of this world, are driven to distraction, are fallible, gullible, in need of repentance. When this rumpus has been tidied up and everyone has had the grace to admit their mistakes, there will be a great deal of forgiving to do, and it will come harder if we lose our tempers now.

Will He? – Won't He?

22 May 1982

Any Catholics who have been playing 'He will come – he won't come' with their rosaries for the past few weeks will, I am sure, be forgiven. It has been almost as nerve-racking as 'They will invade – they won't invade', and of course intimately connected. How to disconnect them has been one of the problems: how to make it psychologically possible for the Pope to visit Britain without seeming either to endorse whatever we may be up to in the South Atlantic or to imply that the waging of war is a trivial sideline that can be ignored. But plainly, the Pope (of all people) cannot ignore it: from the very start of his pontificate, he has been saying (in just so many words), 'Stop the international arms trade! Stop killing one another!' Come to that, he has also told the Latin American juntas to stop oppressing their peoples. The fact that he is ignored is not likely to discourage him from saying it again.

The arguments for and against the visit have been very finely balanced. In spite of every effort to purge the visit of political overtones and to emphasize its pastoral and ecumenical aspects – well, how would *we* feel if the Pope were now in Argentina, blessing crowds of flag-waving Argentines, comforting the widows of war casualties, caught up – willy nilly – in scenes of triumph or tragedy? These may be very hard to avoid in the next ten days. On the other hand, the argument put to Rome by the British Catholic leaders has been that a refusal to come to Britain would be seen by our people as a reproach to Britain, as disapproval, even punishment. If the tragedy, the sinfulness of war is rolling on its way – isn't that precisely the moment when the Supreme Pontiff should stand up and preach the prophetic word to us all, whether we like it or not and whatever bruising the Church may take as a result? But again, there are those in Rome who are more cautious. There are also some who would think it unseemly for a papal visit to be hopelessly upstaged by a war: frankly, it would ruin the whole atmosphere.

It is impossible to ignore the waste of money and materials that cancellation would involve. The feeling among the Catholic hierarchy is that it would take years for the community to build up to that pitch again, psychologically as well as financially. But, at its heart, the Christian faith *is* about coping with failure – bringing something positive out of the negative – and over the past week I have been impressed by the thinking, talking and planning that has gone on to salvage as much as possible from the programme in the event of cancellation; to make it, not *Hamlet* without the Prince, but a different kind of play that is still worth attending. As one priest remarked to me: 'Even if the wedding is off, the family can still cheer itself up with a party.'

Here and there I have met people who hoped – discreetly – that the net result might be a more modest, less triumphalist programme altogether, with or without the Pope: something that would seem less of a confrontation to liberal Protestants and liberal Romans. The latter are not too keen to be thumped over the head with some of the Pope's views on contraception, divorce and married priests; and the former are worried that he may turn the heads of the Anglican Catholics and set back the cause of church unity among the non-Romans.

Which may sound like going too far in the direction of making a virtue out of loss.The vast majority of Roman

Catholics would give anything to have the Pope in their midst, the Holy Father of that universal family to which they belong as well as belonging to this country. But what has struck me, moving in Catholic circles of late, is the extent to which the Roman Catholic Church in Britain is now British, with much the same style of life as the rest of us, and much the same variety (from radical left to conservative right) as the Church of England. With or without the Pope, the next ten days will be an opportunity for it to come into the open and stand confidently on its own feet and show what it is made of.

Habemus Papam

29 May 1982

So, *Habemus Papam* – We have a Pope – and I will admit that I, among others, had not believed for the past seven weeks that he really would come. In an age when everybody, from football players to heads of state, calculates the political consequences of every move, I had forgotten there might still be one man who could determine 'Nevertheless, this I must do'. Which is not to say that Pope John Paul's mission must be exempt from criticism: only that here is a messenger who is prepared to take the consequences of bringing us the news he *has* to bring.

As Cardinal Hume pointed out the other day, events make it inevitable that the mission cannot be entirely otherworldly. It won't do to pretend that when the Pope speaks of peace he means only spiritual peace: he means the ending of warfare in the South Atlantic and the reconciliation of Britain and Argentina. At his mass for the British and Argentine cardinals, he told them 'Peace is not only a duty – it is also possible', and he went on, 'It is impossible not to flinch in terror at the prospects of death and destruction contained in any war today: even if it is waged with so-called conventional weapons which have been endowed by modern technology with a deadly power to devastate and exterminate . . .' That kind of talk could, I suppose, be resented as undermining our national will to win. And yet we all know it is true – every day we can see it getting truer – and if we had taken its warning seriously from the start, we would have left the Argentine aggressors on the Falklands, swallowed our pride and retrieved what we could by a different (and perhaps less costly) route. It seems pretty clear from the opinion polls that most people – including the government – were not impressed by that prospect, and were prepared to face the terror along with our brave forces, even though we have never known (and still do not know) what the consequences will be. Yet somebody must point this out, and who more objective in doing so than the Pope? He certainly cannot be criticized for being naïve about tyranny and torture, which he has opposed as vigorously as he has war and the arms trade.

So what good can the Pope's peace talk do? How many divisions can *he* land? – the Swiss Guard? Come to think of it, papal administration of the Falklands might offer a way out, though a surprising reversion to the temporal power which modern popes have renounced. But short of that, I think we have to see papal intervention (for that is what is going on, despite denials of any political involvement) in psychological as well as spiritual terms.

This is a pastoral visit – the shepherd visiting his Roman Catholic sheep, though he has no objection whatever to other sheep joining in. Many of these sheep are angry, panicky, obsessed with a single view of the world. To the earthly shepherd (as indeed to his heavenly master) sheep are sheep, whatever their breed. They need calming down, their minds raised to a higher level where, perhaps, they can realize their fundamental unity with each other and their common dependence upon the pastures of this earth. Not a bad image to conjure up from the Falklands.

There will still be some listeners (if they have not switched off in Protestant disgust) who will persist in seeing John Paul as a scarlet woman rather than a universal shepherd. Which is a pity! For whether you regard him as utterly infallible or (like most British Catholics) politely pick and choose among what he teaches, there is no substitute for him as the prophetic voice of Christendom. The Bible? Yes, but the Bible would not exist without the Church, and the Bible has always needed interpreting and preaching. With due respect to Dr Billy Graham and the Reverend Ian Paisley, there is no other figure whose office and personality combine so powerfully to say what has to be said. Not being a Catholic myself, I can afford to say, 'Never mind about divorce, contraception or the Real Presence.' What matters fundamentally is the message to Britons and Argentines alike: 'In Christ's name, turn back, O Man, forswear thy foolish ways.'

Thou Art Peter

5 June 1982

For the past two months, the BBC Radio Newsroom has been operating a special War Desk. Last week, a rival unit was set up on the floor below to handle the flood of papal news, and was promptly named the Peace Desk. Ribald communiqués were exchanged between the two, claiming to have captured or recaptured command of the news. 'We are planning a major assault with hymns, blessings, popemobiles and screaming Poles', announced the Peace Desk. 'War should belong to the tragic past . . .'

It was quoting, of course, from John Paul himself, who never let a day go by without making it clear that his visit to Britain was a peace mission as much as anything else. After all the hesitation about coming at all, that effect was enhanced by the very contrast of the spectacle with the war news surrounding it. Whom else – general, prime minister or monarch – would so many people, especially young people, have turned out to see? Perhaps, having seen their faces on television, the cynics and unbelievers should ask themselves what they have been missing.

John Paul's most significant statement was made at Coventry: 'Today the scale and horror of modern warfare – whether nuclear or not – makes it totally unacceptable as a means of settling differences between nations . . . It should find no place on humanity's agenda for the future.' So much for the theory of the Just War. And the Pope added: 'Men and women . . . long for justice. Yes, but for justice filled with mercy.' He could have made those remarks equally well in Argentina – and did so.

The denunciation of war, however, did not obscure the pastoral nature of the mission – its message to the Roman Catholics of Britain. It is not so long since they were regarded as an immigrant church of bog priests and Irish navvies, with an upper crust that was almost a secret society. That is a long way from the truth today; and it seems to me that a major purpose of the papal visit was to celebrate the 'coming out' of English, Scottish and Welsh Catholicism: to help give it the confidence to demonstrate that Catholics are now as British as anyone else, as normal a part of our society as Anglicans, Methodists or Presbyterians, if rather more disciplined. The Pope even respected the variety among them, tactfully refraining from hammering issues like contraception, celibacy or women priests while he was among the more liberal English, but getting tougher as he joined the more conservative Scots. Clearly he had been well briefed by his bishops, and he never failed to pay tribute to the local saints and martyrs wherever he went.

But it must be the third, ecumenical, purpose of the visit that for non-Romans has been most strikingly served. The spearhead of this points towards reunion with the Anglicans; a thrust which was showing signs of tiredness as it ran into the ultimate obstacles: the authority of the papacy itself, the validity of Anglican orders, the dogmas about Mary, and the sharing of Communion. Yet another International Commission is to be set up to worry away at these, and the job will not be easy. But it will be a commission of new and fresher men, and behind it the clergy and laity, Roman and Anglican alike, are charged to adopt every possible means of collaboration.

The significant gesture is at the very heart of the Church – almost the only institution which is prepared to meet this intensely human need. That is what sacraments are all about, and it was the thread holding together the necklace of papal events. I believe that at Canterbury, and again at Liverpool Anglican Cathedral, all Christians were offered a sacrament in the spectacle of the Pope being received, with good will and welcome, by the bishops and people of a church which he in return visibly acknowledged as worthy. Though the arguments remain, at a higher level those encounters made nonsense of them. John Paul can be in no doubt about the dignity and seriousness of our churches, and we should be in no doubt about his. Among other things, he has shown himself a magnificent preacher of the faith. Now it is up to the people to show their impatience – or, I suppose, indifference.

Praying for Peace

12 June 1982

'It must be hard times for you religious people', said a sceptical friend of mine. 'You have been praying your knees off for peace, and not only does the Falklands thing go on regardless – Lebanon gets beaten up, too. And the faster the Pope turns pacifist (as he seems to be doing), the fiercer the fighting gets. You must be tempted to give it all up, or at least convert to Hinduism.'

My friend – my learned friend – was referring to that noble and ancient scripture, the Bhagavad Gita, which tells how Prince Arjuna, about to ride into battle, is sickened at the thought of having to slay his own kith and kin; but is finally persuaded by the God Krishna (disguised as his charioteer) that a warrior must follow his destiny, dispassionately. Which is, I suppose, an honourable philosophy, if hardly a Christian one. It is more like Stoicism, which I have always felt was the natural religion of the English gentleman, rather than Christianity.

But to return to the matter of prayer: what my friend said is all too true. Not even the Pope's Mass for Peace, concelebrated by the cardinals of Britain and Argentina, has abated the conflict. One may question whether, in fact, we have prayed hard enough for peace: I know of few churches which have maintained a constant vigil. But if it is the will of God that man should not kill man – and how could it be otherwise? – that will has not been done, however devoutly prayed for.

The obvious conclusion is that there is no God; or that, if there is one, he is not worth praying to; and that the only prayers that are answered are those which are going to be fulfilled anyway. I think there is a grain of truth in that – for in 'Thy will be done' we are taught that one function of prayer is to bring us to accept God's will. It is pagan, not Christian, to think of prayer as the manipulation of God with magic spells: changing his mind by uttering the right words. I am also sure that we do wrong to suppose that God is the God of Victory, awarding success to those who make the right gestures. Certainly God has a will for us. But, as I have argued before, he grants us the freedom to ignore it and think we know better. As a result of which, we carry on crucifying ourselves and him. He suffers as we suffer – that is one meaning of the Crucifixion.

So let nobody imagine that when human beings tear each other apart, in the Middle East or the South Atlantic, it conclusively proves that God is either nonexistent or indifferent to our fate. On the contrary, it confirms that he has entered so totally into our lives that he is at our mercy; ignored, mocked, flogged and tormented to death. Though, being God, he rises again and demands: I am still with you – where do we go from here?

So, when we pray for peace, we are not conjuring God to wave a magic wand and give us victory on our terms. Our prayers for peace cannot seek to impose conditions on God: we cannot pray 'Give us peace *after* we have liberated Port Stanley, or wiped out the PLO'. There is no Holy War – there never was – nor are we wise enough to know how far we can go without causing more suffering than we have cured. That is not to dishonour the soldier – for him, Arjuna's course is the only course: but he is the victim as well as the executioner.

Is there still any point in praying for peace? I think there is, for two reasons. Prayer, above all, is listening rather than pestering. It is the one chance we give God to tell us personally what *he* thinks; the one chance to lay the problem before him, helplessly and penitently, and seek the way out – or at least the way in which we can make something positive out of the mess we have created. Second – and here I may seem to be making God too human (which in many ways he is) – but God needs our sympathy and support. He hangs there, bleeding to death, and if all he can hear is the cry for more blood, then we shall be guilty of something like the despair of God.

Pax Vobiscum

19 June 1982

So it seems to be over in the Falklands, and God be thanked – or rather, apologized to. Whether the Pope or our prayers had anything to do with the end of this war, I could not presume to say; and nothing I have said or shall say can detract from the courage and skill of those who won it. One of my hopes, when it all began, was that if there had to be a war, it could be fought cleanly and with chivalry – that it would not degenerate into indiscriminate slaughter, as World War Two did. And it is to the high credit of our leaders and commanders in the field that (with very few exceptions indeed) it did not degenerate. Perhaps the peace movement has had that effect, at least: that a great tenderness has been shown over matters like casualties, not expanding the conflict, the prompt return of prisoners of war. And under the circumstances, the death toll has been remarkably small. For all of this our leaders deserve, as I say, the highest credit.

Which is not to say that I am changing my tune and endorsing what has been done. In some ways we have been extremely lucky, and in others very foolish. The foolishness will be subject to political investigation, and we can (I hope) be confident that our newfound awareness of the evils of fascist dictatorship – an awareness so lacking in the early 1930s – will be vigorously applied to our foreign policies in future; as, no doubt, will the lessons to be drawn from selling arms round the world as if they were Leyland buses. But it is to be hoped that our luck will not be overlooked either: just a few more Exocets in the wrong place, a nuclear bomb or two in the wrong hands, and we should have been wringing our hands instead of the church bells. Nor, because the casualties have been relatively light, does it mean that the action has been less frightful for those involved. War is not fun when you are in it. War remains Hell, even if you win.

We do not actually know – and nobody can calculate – what the long-term effects of our victory will be. The one reliable principle of history is its inscrutability, and with all our sophistication and intelligence, we live from moment to moment. In ten years' time we may see things in a very different light, just as we do the Suez adventure. My colleague Christopher Wain has laid out just about every possibility from Argentina joining the Soviet bloc, to Britain keeping East Falkland and Argentina getting the less desirable West. Neither is quite what we thought we were fighting for.

But first there will be medals and awards. I should like to think there was some recognition for the BBC's men Fox and Hanrahan, for managing (against fearful odds) to communicate just what it was like to be at war. If we resisted jingoism – and I think we generally did as a broadcasting organization – it was largely because they made it impossible.

So what has been proved? Something of military value; things yet unknown of economic and political significance;

and two very sad conclusions for the family of Man, God's children. First, that war as an attempt at solving disputes is alive and well and thriving in Britain and Argentina: there was a chance to renounce it, but that chance was rejected, and the military option remains very much alive for the future. The next aggressor will have to be better equipped, and so will we, no doubt, at whatever cost. The second sad thing is that the United Nations, upon which the churches had pinned all their hopes for eliminating war, remains basically flawed and futile: it was actually in position in southern Lebanon, and before we reproach it for not having stopped Israel, why could it do nothing to stop the provocation against which Israel reacted? The answer is that no member – including ourselves – is prepared to put our faith in an authority which may not see us as we see ourselves. We would rather have it helpless. We would rather see it crucified.

Yours Finally

26 June 1982

Good morning – and goodbye. Yesterday I retired from the BBC, and this is the last talk in this series that I have been asked to give. Seeing that they have been running for the past five years and that I have never once been censored by my bosses, that's given me a pretty good run for your money – including those of you who've detested every word. Time, perhaps, for a different point of view. For nobody is irreplaceable; there are many ways of looking at God, and it matters less that you should agree with what you hear than that you should be stimulated to find your own image of him.

I've never agreed with the notion that we in the mass media exercise great influence. The people who write claiming that we do always point out that we haven't fooled *them*. If we are lucky, we manage to express what some people are thinking already but hadn't quite articulated, and that, I suppose, gives them courage and comfort. But equally, we can show them what they *don't* believe. The delicacy of the job lies in knowing how to tell people what they would rather not hear without hurting or insulting them. As I said when I first began this series: if I offend, please forgive me.

And, as I've said many times since, the greatest reward has been the correspondence that has poured in quite beyond my capacity to answer adequately. There can't be many journalists who can use their public as their principal source material; but I have learnt more about the condition of faith today from my letters than I have from any synod or seminar. I am very much obliged to you for it.

One thing I had not expected when I took up this job, and that's what you might call the 'pastoral aspect' of it: the letters asking for help about doctrine, advice about morals, information about everything from book titles to retreat houses. The gravest responsibility of all – and one which I've neither sought nor been qualified for – has been coping with cries for help from people near suicide, or those in great misery, like the woman who for more than sixty years had been tormented by the fear that her unbaptized baby was in limbo. For one reason or another, there is this vast Church of the Unchurched out there, believing profoundly in the world of the spirit, but unable to connect it with the institutional churches. They are essentially religious, but they will not be dragooned into religion. Perhaps in me they have been able to recognize their own apprehension that there is a God, but also their own independence and doubts about categorical dogma. We're in the absurd position where people like me have the pulpit but not the authority, while the churches which claim the authority have lost the pulpit. How we bridge the gap, I wish I knew. I do not think the answer is to play more gospel songs on the radio, or to paste up gospel texts on the London Underground.

I think the decline in the churches has 'bottomed out', as they say. Some have even turned upwards a bit. I do actually believe in the churches, for all their faults, for faith needs some structure, and we all need societies of friends, communities that care for one another all the week round. If I were obliged to rough out a blueprint for the Church of the future, I would start with the need for good popular theology, to affirm that God exists and what he is like, and upon this try to effect a renewal of religious education, at all ages. Next, I would drag the laity deeper and deeper into ministry of all kinds, joining lay orders, popping in and out of monasteries, preaching, healing, celebrating irregular eucharists, too, I hope. Finally, since human organization demands leadership, we must get bishops (or moderators) back to what they were in the Celtic Church – not committee men and administrators, but evangelists and saints. I know some very holy bishops even today, but they find it hard to fit in their diaries.

My diary says it is time for me to move on. I've enjoyed being here, but if a caravan rests too long in one place, it gets bogged down. Nunc dimittis . . . I remain, yours faithfully . . .

Enjoying God's Creation

For BBC Radio Medway, Lent 1982

> The spacious firmament on high,
> With all the blue ethereal sky,
> And spangled heavens, a shining frame,
> Their Great Original proclaim . . .

Despite the enthusiasm with which Joseph Addison wrote those lines the Universe is an ambiguous place. It is easy enough to enjoy it in its kinder moments, but there are many people who scarcely enjoy it at all. For everyone who finds God on a country walk, there is another who looks upon a malformed baby and demands 'What kind of demon can allow such suffering? Is this the work of an omnipotent Creator who allows the innocent to perish in earthquakes, famine and plagues?' Such people lapse either into a vehement atheism, or into a resignation that the world is meaningless and absurd.

Before we can talk about Enjoying God the Creator, we've got to be sure that there *is* a God, and in what sense he's responsible for Creation. Three people in every four say that they believe in God – but often he is just a vague principle made up of the laws of gravity, electricity and thermodynamics with a pinch of 'See that ye love one another' to sweeten the brew. That is not the Christian God (or the Muslim or Jewish God, either): we believe in a personal God – that is, a God who treats us as persons and who makes himself known to us as a person. How can you prove the existence of such a God? I don't think you can, not if you want the sort of logical, measurable proof required by science. I can prove there is a cat in the garden by going and picking it up and showing it has all the scientific characteristics of a cat. But you cannot do that with God – you can't even say what the characteristics of a God would be if you found one. If there is a God, we would expect him to be beyond our powers to define. But that does not mean there is not one, or that there cannot be one. Why do we keep using the word, if it does not stand for anything? Why have people always behaved *as if* there were a God? Why do they have this instinct for him, if there is nothing there? Human beings haven't been idiots for a hundred thousand years and suddenly come to their senses in the last one hundred. It really would have been 'meaningless and absurd' for them to have been sending up their prayers all this time if they got nothing back. That is one vital clue: those who believe in him do get something back in return, and they know it.

That still is not scientific proof. And although I said we cannot prove his existence scientifically (he is much too clever for that), there are countless pointers in his direction. There is something 'out there' – and, just as important, 'in here' – which is powerful and inexplicable. And however many explanations we try to offer scientifically, they do not touch the real mystery of God. He is always behind them, beyond them, above them. Not contradicting them, though; always in tune with them and (I should say) rather proud of them. Would not you be proud if you had been responsible for the double-helix of DNA, the coding system that enables a single cell to grow into a complex human body with all its nerves and bones and muscles?

But was he responsible? Did he 'create' the double-helix, or did it just happen by chance? Again, I cannot prove it. But nor can anyone possibly prove that it happened by chance – for the chances against that are so colossal that we may as well say it could never happen. And remember, we have to account for a huge number of such miracles (if that is not an unfair word to use here). If we are looking for the simplest and most obvious explanation – which is what atheists usually urge us to do – then it's very hard to avoid God.

Still no proof; and if you are arguing with non-believers it is no good, either, to wave the Bible in their faces crying 'It is all perfectly simple – the Bible *is* true because it *says* it is true'. It may very well be true: but I don't think it is at all simple. I can only say that I do not expect – in this life – to know the answer to everything; but that I find the Christian hypothesis of God works better in my experience than any other – and it has worked not only for me, but for a long chain of witnesses which we may call 'the communion of saints'. I may niggle at some of their details, but basically I believe they are right.

So I don't see anything wrong with Genesis as a grand poem of creation – a poem, not a palaeontological text-book. And I am fascinated, above all, by its insights into the laws of nature and into the origin of sin. There at the beginning, we see the Creator firmly dividing this from that, setting the two great lights to rule the day and the night. He does not just play with his creation to suit his own whims – he establishes orderly systems to run themselves, and thereby he limits his own powers. He is not omnipotent in the sense of being an arbitrary tinkerer with Nature – making the sun rise and set at unpredictable hours, or the rain to fall whenever people pray hard enough for it: no, they have laws to obey – for this is Creation, not Chaos.

And almost as soon as God creates Man, he gives him the power of choice. In the first place, Adam merely chooses the names of the animals; but before long, he is choosing to disobey God's ban on eating from the Tree of the Knowledge of Good and Evil. That means we are able to know the difference between right and wrong and, if we wish, deliberately choose wrong.

God could have created mankind without any such power of choice – without what we call free will. Like the animals, we would simply have been programmed to feed and breed as things befell us; and nobody accuses an animal of sin, because it knows no better – it does what it has to do. Nor (I think) does an animal know God; though I am nervously aware there are some devout animal-lovers who disagree with me about that.

The point is, we could have been programmed by God to do nothing but the best – with no choices to make at all. That would have saved us a lot of trouble, a great deal of suffering. There would have been no sin. But we would then have been God's puppets – Nature's puppets, if you prefer – and I submit such a creature would not have been a human being as we understand it at all. It would not have been worth being, nor, from God's point of view, worth having.

For if God is Love ('Caring' is perhaps a less sentimental word) then that love can only be fully expressed in a relationship with something that can love back. Love, to be fully love, has to be first shown, then recognized for what it is, and then returned – returned freely. If love is to be freely returned, it must be possible for it also to be freely rejected.

That is why God created man and woman with the freedom to love him or reject him – to follow his will for us or to say, 'No – I'd rather do something different' (which usually turns out to be a disaster). Like any parent who really loves his children and doesn't just want to enslave and devour them, God grants us the freedom to make our own mistakes. And again, like any loving parent, when they hurt themselves or each other, he too suffers and grieves with them – as he did on the Cross. He suffers and grieves again when they get caught up in an earthquake which – under the laws of his Creation – *had* to happen; or suffer from lack of rain which – under the laws of his Creation – *could not* fall. And sometimes, when his children die, they die in great pain: for pain is a warning system of some breakdown in the body, and *something* has got to break down if we are to die at all, to make room for others and go on to something better. In a way, people who complain about pain are complaining that we die at all: they want it easy all the way. But total bliss would be total oblivion. No – of course I cannot explain away all the mysteries of suffering: I should be God myself if I could. But I do not think Creation is absurd, and nobody really behaves as if they did. I *do* think we can enjoy it.

Especially since it is much more than, once upon a time, God dividing the light from the darkness, putting Adam and Eve in Eden, and then standing back and letting them make a mess of things. To the Church, to Christians, Creation means the *continuing* created order, and the continuous acts of God's creative love.

Time, I suspect, is the great illusion. Creation did not just happen *then*, long ago, it is happening now; and we are called upon to be God's assistants in it. It could have begun with perfection and stayed like that – stayed in the Garden of Eden. But no, we wanted it the hard way. We thought we knew something better. 'Very well', says God. 'Come out and help me make this world the place it should be. Here's land, here's timber and stone, plants and animals and water: only work *with* my Universe and not against it . . .'

Genesis shows this very clearly, and it is reaffirmed in God's promises to Noah, and by the experience of ordinary Christians to whom God repeats it every morning. We do not have to lie back, fatalistically, and wait for the undertaker: there is always something creative for us to do.

This amazing privilege calls for our action in response. To enjoy Creation is not merely to relax in it: it is to be fired by joy, to rejoice, to be stirred into expressing our joy in action. For we are responsible – more than ever, today – for the care and protection of what God creates, and that includes ourselves and each other. Already we have exhausted too much of what was entrusted to us: whole races have been wiped out, whole species of animals, whole ecological systems. Enjoying Creation has been confused with exploiting it heedlessly, guzzling it up like a free banquet.

I am not one of those who would put the clock back to a mythical age of rustic simplicity. I actually believe that the aeroplane, the car, the telephone (even television) are derived from the creative spirit of God and are intended for the good of his children, just as are the creative arts, like music, poetry or painting. Without God's laws of nature, they would not work. What matters here is, can we *enjoy* them, can we use them to God's glory, or do we forget that they have been put at our service to further God's will? Do we allow them to become an end in themselves? That is the great heresy: to worship the created instead of the Creator.

Above all, it seems to me, Creation means the continuous making of mankind – in which, again, we are invited to join. We are called into life to help make ourselves, our children, our neighbours and our whole society – if need be, to improve them. And I dare say (in spite of some catastrophic lapses in recent times) that we *have* made some progress: we do treat women, children, servants and employees of all kinds far better than we did centuries ago. The very fact that we are worried, for example, about the Third World shows that we have some sense of where the Creative spirit is trying to lead us.

We are told that God has created us 'in his own image', which is a startling and apparently naïve assertion. 'Do you really believe God is an old man with a long white beard?' the scientific disbeliever demands. Well, of course I don't. But he is infinitely adaptable. The last time he was around, he picked the form of a young Galilean Jew. Christians call it 'The Incarnation' – God coming into flesh – and just as Creation was not just once but forever, so Incarnation is permanently with us, making the human body the one true temple of God. 'Lo, he abhors not the Virgin's womb' – he is not too high and almighty to inhabit his Creation. I and my Quaker friends speak of 'that of God in every one'; and that tells us there is nobody – no matter how unattractive on the outside – who should not be approached without reverence for that scrap of Christ within them. It is to that scrap that we should speak.

I may seem to be talking a kind of humanism – to be exalting the dignity of sinful mankind – and in a sense, I am. I believe (with the great theologian Hans Küng) that to be a Christian is to be truly human. It is not – as some people imagine – to be piously inhuman, to anaesthetize half of our being.

God did not create an evil creature, and I think it is blasphemy to suggest that he did. He created a good creature with the free will to go wrong. Never forget, though, that we also have the power to know God's will and go right. Thus, if we are to enjoy one another – to see one another at our best – we are most likely to find that enjoyment among people who know God's will rather than just their own. The most enjoyable of all are those whose vision of themselves actually coincides with God's vision of them. Sometimes they have ascertained it through struggle and prayer. Sometimes it comes instinctively, and you will find it in people who do not consciously profess God at all. In such people you will find an absence of inner conflict, a glad acceptance of what they are. They have accepted their true and God-given nature, which is the best in them.

Does that sound too much like life in a monastery? Well, monks and nuns do have the opportunity – and the hard work – of listening for God's will, trying to detect which way the wind of the Holy Spirit is blowing. The greatest obstacle to the life of faith today is the sheer uproar, busy-ness and complexity of our life. The current of Creation – of what God is seeking our co-operation to make – flows very deep. It is blotted out by the flotsam and jetsam we dump on the surface (and we are afraid to dive deep). If only we can clear the rubbish away, dive deep and go with that current, we shall find the ride exhilarating. We can enjoy it.

I must return, though, to the lonely and frustrated who see very little to rejoice about in Creation: no career that fitted them, no beauty in their lives, no gratitude, no exhilaration. Tell some of *them* to accept what they are, and you'll get some very bitter replies.

Too often, I am afraid, such people are the victims of a poor creative effort by the rest of us. Parents, friends and children have ignored God's will that they should flourish and grow, and, instead, they have been left to wither away. We all know such people: but do we ever ask what part *we* have played in making them the way they are, what part we have played in creating them, what part we might play in their resurrection? We have to remember, too, that the Creator, whose will we so constantly frustrate, forgives, forgives endlessly: otherwise he would destroy. So we, too, can only create if we forgive – forgive others and ourselves. Only then can we enjoy ourselves and others.

All Creation dies; and we must – if we are to enjoy

Creation – forgive that, too. It is the law, to which there cannot be exceptions, and it is necessary. I generalize here, and generalizations are of no comfort to the bereaved: how can I find God's purpose in the cot-death of a baby, or the road-death of a young husband? I do not presume to. I really doubt if he willed it; and I am sure he grieves too, and looks desperately for some creative outcome of that destruction. What we have to do, as soon as we have the strength, is to join him in that search. For by the surrender of his power involved in Creation, God has rendered himself surprisingly weak. His only power is love, and he cannot go on without our help, our love. So, let us embrace it – let us enjoy it.